WINTER
WISE

WINTER WISE

TRAVEL AND SURVIVAL IN ICE AND SNOW

Monty Alford

VICTORIA · VANCOUVER · CALGARY

Heritage House Publishing Company Ltd.
heritagehouse.ca

LIBRARY AND ARCHIVES CANADA CATALOGUING IN PUBLICATION

Alford, Monty, 1923–, author
    Winter wise : travel and survival in ice and snow / Monty Alford.

Issued in print and electronic formats.
ISBN 978-1-927527-40-5 (pbk.).—ISBN 978-1-926936-84-0 (epub).—ISBN 978-1-927051-63-4 (pdf)

    1. Wilderness survival. 2. Snow camping. I. Title.

GV200.5.A435 2013   613.6'9   C2013-903377-7   C2013-903378-5

Edited by Jill Fallis (first edition) and Lara Kordic (second edition)
Proofread by Will Johnson
Cover and book design by Jacqui Thomas
Cover photos: gaspr13/iStockphoto.com (*front*); jcarillet/iStockphoto.com (*back*)
Photo on page 150: kongzinzhu/iStockphoto.com

Distributed in the U.S. by Publishers Group West

 The interior of the book was produced on 30% post-consumer recycled paper, processed chlorine-free and printed with vegetable-based inks.

Heritage House acknowledges the financial support for its publishing program from the Government of Canada through the Canada Book Fund (CBF), Canada Council for the Arts, and the Province of British Columbia through the British Columbia Arts Council and the Book Publishing Tax Credit.

17 16 15 14 13   1 2 3 4 5

Printed in Canada

IT WAS IN ORDER to pursue my obligations as a hydrometric surveyor working through many Yukon winters that I had the opportunity to experience the mystical world of ice and snow in all its forms. Not only did the ice-covered rivers and lakes provide a convenient travel and work platform, but the snow covering the land could be used to build a shelter and melted in a receptacle to provide drink.

The disadvantage of such exposure to the white world was that I was frequently away from my home and family. With my deep gratitude for enduring those absences and for their unflagging support I dedicate this handbook to my dear wife Renée and our six children.

CONTENTS

~

INTRODUCTION

~

THIS IS A HANDBOOK for all who travel, by whatever means, in isolated regions in the colder parts of the world at the coldest time of year. It is a guide for the ski or snowshoe traveller, the snowmobiler, the dog musher and the winter motorist.

It is during that period, 'twixt **freeze-up** and **breakup**, when snow blankets the land and the lakes and rivers are frozen, that wilderness travellers can go just about anywhere. Swamps are solid, and regions of frost-shattered rock (felsenmeer) have been smoothed by a blanket of snow. Ski and snowshoe travellers are able to break trail from forest to frozen lake or river surface without breaking stride. Snowmobile operators can do the same without rising from their seat.

There is, of course, a price to pay for such freedom, and that is an exposure to sub-zero temperatures with the attendant risk of hypo-thermia, frostbite, or falling through thin ice. This manual includes sections on how the body reacts to cold, how to dress for cold, and how to safely use a frozen river or lake as a pathway.

The vital questions that all winter travellers must ask themselves is whether they have the know-how and equipment to survive should they be unexpectedly marooned. Day travellers must be prepared for the possibility of being benighted without the benefit of a sleeping bag. Are you able to build an effective emergency shelter? Do you know how to light a fire if kindling is available? Are you carrying a **personal survival kit** (PSK) that contains a means of melting snow to provide warm drinks? If the answer to any of these questions is no, then this handbook should be of interest and importance to you.

While some of the information related to wilderness travel presented here may be found in other manuals, the data pertaining to travel on ice surfaces comes mostly from my experiences, both happy and unhappy, as a hydrometric surveyor, wilderness traveller, and mountaineer who has lived, worked, and played in Canada's Yukon for the past sixty-two years. What further sets this book apart are the original designs for items such as an ice chisel, ice prod, ice dagger, portable open-terrain sled, and, most importantly, candle stove (YuCan). The YuCan stove is an essential feature of the **personal survival kit**. This kit should be carried at all times when travelling beyond ready help and distant from warm shelter.

Reports and statistics reveal that many wilderness travellers have perished for want of a little knowledge and a few crucial items. My hope is that this handbook will help you have a safe journey. May the wonders of winter never fail to beckon and may all your travels and explorations be pleasant and rewarding.

chapter 1

LIVING WITH ICE AND SNOW

THE CLOSER YOU GET to the geographical poles the more the snow, ice, and temperature will influence your life. Such elements will affect the way you travel, dress, and think. Those indigenous people who live in the high latitudes, including the Samoyeds of Siberia, the Inuit of Canada, and the Sami of Scandinavia, have become one with this ever-challenging environment. The penetrating cold and wind, the days of darkness, the splendour of the aurora borealis, and the ever-dominating canopy of white over the land have become to such people the essential matrix of life. As *Homo sapiens,* a species anatomically designed for subtropical regions, circumpolar peoples have adapted well to living in the most hostile environments on the planet.

Winter is a time of contrast. There can be fierce winds and low temperatures, or an uncanny stillness and chilly, but not biting, winds. The pervasive white blanket underfoot serves as a flat screen showing myriad black lines, the shadows of tree trunks, which appear long because of the low sun. In some locations, where the trees are sparse and snow-laden, they are often sculpted by the wind to make pedestals of great beauty that rest the roving eye.

To outdoor enthusiasts the arrival of snow is manna from heaven since it promises a challenging and invigorating environment that will enhance our recreational freedom. To others it means clearing driveways, motoring on slippery roads, worrying about avalanches on certain highways, and bundling up children. In other words, it is a darned nuisance. If we add the occurrence of unexpected snow and ice storms, high winds, and blinding blizzards that result in road closures and power outages, especially if such meteorological events are foreign to the region and people are unprepared, then such conditions can be life-threatening. Anyone planning a wilderness experience in fall or winter must make special preparations for the journey.

We are often tempted to get in that last canoe trip before the river or lake freezes.

While the temperatures of fall may not be extremely low, the combination of rain and wind at this time of year imposes the need for sufficient attire to protect us from hypothermia. Wet and cold can be as threatening as −20°C temperatures. Have we equipment to guarantee that we can light a fire when all our wood is wet? Does our tent have a good fly? Is our spare clothing and sleeping bag carried in a waterproof bag? As my uncle used to say, "Hope for the best, plan for the worst, and take what comes with a smile."

Despite the sombre pictures so readily conjured up by the words of Yukon bard Robert Service ("The Spell of the Yukon") and storyteller Jack London ("To Build a Fire"), winter is a season that has much more to offer than discomfort and torment. Let us consider the pros and cons.

ADVANTAGES OF WINTER TRAVEL

* Tracks in the snow remind us that we are not alone, while our own tracks help us navigate and can be a guide for the return journey, provided they have not been obscured by drifted snow.

* The hard, wind-carved, wave-like snow surfaces (sastrugi) encountered on plateaus are often monodirectional, which helps us maintain a straight course.

* You can slide things on a snow or ice surface. Travelling on skis can be faster than travelling on foot over the same terrain in summer. You can pull your gear on a sled or toboggan instead of toting a heavy pack. Better still, you can use a dog team to make quick, non-mechanized progress.

* Travel by ski, snowshoe, or snow machine is easier in winter because roots, deadfalls, and small bushes are covered by a deep layer of snow.

* Frozen rivers and lakes can offer a level and unobstructed surface on which to travel. We can go places in winter that we can't reach in summer without a boat.

* Muskeg can be readily crossed in winter because it is frozen.

* Drinking water is everywhere, provided we have the means to melt snow or ice.

* Potential shelter-building material is all around us if we know how to construct a snow shelter.

* Bears are in hibernation during winter, so unwanted encounters are less likely (however, we could encounter polar bears if our route borders the Arctic Ocean).

* There are no harassing insects in winter.

* We may view the spectacular aurora borealis.

* The chance of forest fire is minimal.

DISADVANTAGES OF WINTER TRAVEL

* We are deprived of the opportunity to view plant life.

* There are far fewer birds to observe.

* There is an absence of colour.

* There is a short daylight period, or none at all at certain times of year above the Arctic Circle.

* Below-freezing temperatures make it more difficult to maintain our critical 37°C body core temperature and increase our risk of developing hypothermia.

* There is a chance of frostbite.

* There is a chance of snow blindness.

* We require more clothing and equipment in winter than we do in spring and summer. Special tools are required to measure ice thickness, and we should be equipped with safety and rescue equipment in case we fall through an ice cover.

* To take advantage of the surface of frozen lakes and rivers for travel we should be aware of the different types of ice and the load-bearing strength of specific ice thicknesses.

A young Vuntut Gwitchin woman has cut blocks of snow from a hard drift on the bank of the Porcupine River at Old Crow, Yukon. These will be hauled on the toboggan to her house for domestic use.

chapter 2

~

ICE

ICE CAN BE INSPIRATIONAL and beautiful when we view it as a natural phenomenon in the form of a frozen waterfall, glacier, iceberg, or in the dynamic process of formation as it covers a river or lake. It is usually the expansive frozen surfaces of the latter that offer a new freedom to winter travellers who may use skis, snowshoes, or snowmobiles to reach new and far vistas.

At this point we must introduce a warning. To use frozen water as a pathway without understanding the processes of ice formation, growth, and bearing strength would be folly indeed. This section will give you information that will contribute to your safety as you make use of such a floating platform.

It is an unfortunate reality that many people who travel willy-nilly across frozen rivers and lakes do so without knowing how ice forms, grows, and decays. Most travellers do not know where danger areas are or how much ice can support the load they intend to place upon it. Nor do they know what techniques to use to better the chance of safe passage. There is no such thing as a guarantee of safety on any ice cover. The load-bearing potential of any ice is unpredictable, especially on rivers, due to it being considerably less uniform in thickness than lake ice.

WALKING ON WATER

This handbook complements other fine books that deal with wilderness and winter survival by paying specific attention to ice and snow as travel platforms. If you use appropriate safety measures and travel techniques, frozen water can be used not only as a winter playground for recreational use but as a highway to allow the freighting of supplies to isolated northern settlements. Some villages that are accessible only by air depend on the annual formation of ice roads to allow tankers and freight trucks to bring heavy supplies. Snow, like ice, can be used as a surface on which to travel when it blankets frozen muskeg.

We have to begin with an understanding of how ice forms, how there can be good (safe) ice surfaces and bad (dangerous) ones. We should also have the right equipment to measure ice thickness and know how to read the ice surface just as a river boatman reads the water surface.

THE FORMATION PROCESS

There are two fundamental facts that we must keep firmly in mind before we leave terra firma:

1. Any ice cover is continually undergoing a process of metamorphosis.

2. To have any bearing strength at all the ice *has* to be supported by water.

To start at the beginning, when water is cooled it contracts (like most things do) until it reaches 4°C (39°F), at which point—the point of maxium density, when the specific gravity of water is greater than at any other time—it starts to expand.

The fact that water expands upon cooling from 4°C to 0°C (39°F to 32°F) is a significant natural phenomenon. To be a little more specific, as a sheet of fresh water is cooled, the upper layers become more and more dense; they then sink and the displaced water is forced to the surface where it, in turn, is cooled. This process continues until the mass of water has reached 4°C. Further cooling of the surface then causes an expansion of the upper layers until these lighter ones solidify. We now have a **floating** ice cover, which serves as an insulator to prevent the water below it from freezing.

Dare we imagine what would happen if lakes and rivers froze from surface to bed? The heat of the short northern summer would never thaw them, and the environment would be dramatically, in many ways catastrophically, different.

Ice is monomineralic with a hexagonal crystal having an A and C axis. The A axis grows rapidly, first in a horizontal direction and then, finding no room (ice cover), it turns slowly to vertical. These vertical crystals have their largest cross-section at the base.

Remnant candle ice forced upon the riverbank during breakup.

It is during the spring melt (decay) of the ice cover that we can best observe these crystals (often referred to as candles) in remnant ice along lake shorelines or riverbanks immediately after breakup.

Types of Ice

Anchor Ice — This type of ice is an early winter phenomenon. It forms on clear, cold nights as a result of temperature depression caused by heat loss from radiation. Anchor ice generally rises from the stream bed after sunrise to join the frazil ice running on the surface.

Black Ice (also referred to as Blue Ice) — This is the most pure and dense form of ice and, for that reason, the strongest. The term is a misnomer since the ice is transparent; the colour comes from the dark water on which it floats.

Candle Ice — Deteriorating, columnar-grained ice is a spring phenomenon. Influenced by warming temperatures and in the process of decay, the formerly solid ice cover becomes transforms into long pencil-like crystals through the melting of inter-crystal films. These crystals slide past each other easily, and ice that is 1 metre (3 feet) thick might not bear the weight of a person.

Frazil Ice — Also called frazil slush, this is ice in suspension in the river and takes the form of small, generally disc-shaped crystals. Fast and turbulent open-water sections in a river favour the formation of frazil. The crystals coalesce and are carried under the permanent ice cover, where they often adhere to its undersurface.

Glacier Ice — Not to be confused with mountain glaciers or polar ice caps, which originate in snowfall, glacier ice describes river glaciation, more technically referred to as **aufeis**. This condition develops when water is forced by channel blockage to run atop the initial ice cover, where it freezes. This happens frequently on small creeks and shallow braided rivers where the channel freezes to the bed. This surface inundation often continues throughout the winter to produce an extensive glaciated area by spring. Such a glacier often remains in place long after the normal breakup date for rivers in that region.

Shelf Ice — This is a layer of ice left in suspension after the supporting water, present during its formation, has withdrawn. It is remnant ice and often flanks a riverbank for some time after the river is open.

White Ice — This ice usually has relatively high air or snow content; its strength depends on its density. High-density white ice has a strength approaching that of clear black ice, but it is opaque. When heavily impregnated with snow crystals and air bubbles, it will become much weaker.

Ice Identification and Metamorphosis

Over a period of time you will subconsciously catalogue those signs that tell you whether particular ice is likely to be safe or not. I refer to such indicators as colour, surface irregularity, texture, and sound. Always be wary of any ice that is white or blotchy, as this is an indication of a loose texture. The ice may have air bubbles or snow mixed with it or both. You are walking on a frozen sponge, which does not have the same bearing strength as clear, dense, blue lake ice. Hold back from any ice cover that emits a hollow sound when you prod it; it is most likely shell ice, which has hardly any bearing capability because it is unsupported by water. Watch too for any mounding, which can indicate a pressure fault on a lake. It is common for pressure ridges to form on a lake to create localized flooding on either side of the ridge and where the ice could be unsafe. Fresh animal tracks are useful indicators of a possible route. If the ice has recently supported a moose or caribou, chances are it will support you. A wet snow cover will warn of the presence of overflow.

Generally speaking the ice cover on rivers and lakes, which generally remain frozen all winter, grows steadily (on the underside) as the season progresses. The actual rate of growth is influenced by the insulating effect of the snow cover; the adhesion of frazil ice to the cover on a river (at the ice–water interface); air temperature; the presence of thermal springs and convection currents; and, in the case of rivers, velocity. While by mid-January there may be 0.5 metre (1.5 feet) of ice, by the end of March at the same location you could find a cover that is 1 metre (3 feet) thick.

Thick or Thin?

On a river the ice will be thickest where there is frazil ice adhering to its underside (a frazil dam to the ice scientist). There are occasions where a frazil dam completely blocks a section of the channel to extend from the ice cover to the stream bed. Ice may also be thick where overflow events have occurred and such an inundation has frozen to the surface of the original cover. An ice cover will invariably be thinnest where the velocity is fastest, often on the outside of bends and where the channel is narrow. It is not uncommon for rivers to remain completely free of ice at locations where there are riffles or rapids.

When spring arrives and the ice begins to respond to a higher, warmer sun, it loses strength rapidly. As soon as the vertical ice crystals can slide past one another, called candling, a thick ice cover will have little or no load-bearing strength.

The periphery of a frozen lake melts first. Heat is reflected from a snow-free shoreline, from any driftwood or other debris that was deposited along the shoreline prior to freeze-up. The result is the creation of a peripheral moat of open water to make the ice cover of the lake a floating island. Crystal decay, a rapid change in the thermocline, and wind contribute to breakup.

Breakup on rivers usually occurs three to four weeks after the mean air temperature has risen above 0°C (32°F). On small streams an opening normally appears at midstream, or where the current is fastest, and gradually widens. On large rivers, continually rising air temperatures combined with increases in water level coming from surface and subsurface (a rise in groundwater release) weaken the bond with the riverbank and allow movement of the entire cover. Breakup often takes place along the course of a river following a sequential series of dramatic ice dams that progress downstream. These ice dams, created by the jamming of huge ice floes at shallow or narrow points, are often of sufficient strength and magnitude to create serious flooding upstream.

Bearing Strength of Ice

Remembering what has been said before about the need for an ice cover to be supported by water in order to bear a load, and that the purest ice is the strongest (predominantly found on a lake and referred to as clear blue, or black, ice) we can now consider the relationship between thickness and bearing strength.

Table 1, showing the bearing strength of various thicknesses of ice, will serve as a frame of reference. It is useful to know that you don't necessarily have to wait for 15 centimetres (6 inches) of ice before taking advantage of its surface as a possible hiking route. For the foot traveller, 7.6 centimetres (3 inches) of blue lake ice could be considered as acceptable, whereas a person using a snowmobile would be wise to wait for 15 centimetres (6 inches). The thicknesses indicated are the *minimum* for the *strongest* ice.

The key to safe travel is keen observation coupled with systematic testing. This procedure is particularly pertinent shortly after freeze-up and pre-breakup, which is the period of candling. Once routes along a river or across a lake have been proven safe in the early winter in latitudes north of 60, they usually remain so until the approach of spring or the arrival of warmer temperatures. It is useful to know that repeated use weakens ice and that ice is strongest at very low temperatures.

TABLE 1 — Bearing Strength of Good, Totally Supported Blue Lake Ice

| Minimum Ice Thickness | | Load (Moving) | Weight | |
centimetres	inches		kilograms	pounds
5	2	single person on skis	—	—
7.6	3	single person on foot	—	—
15	6	recreational snowmobile or ATV	454	1,000
20	8	compact car or light pickup	1,455	3,200
25	10	medium truck	2,272	5,000
30.5	12	medium truck with load	3,636	8,000
38	15	heavy truck	5,454	12,000

Consult your manual for the gross vehicle weight rating (GVWR) of your vehicle. Comparative strength of different types of ice:
 • River ice is 15% weaker than good (blue) lake ice.
 • Sea ice is 50% weaker than clear freshwater lake ice.
For such values to be meaningful, the air temperature should be no higher than -7°C (20°F). Ice is strongest at lower temperatures. Repeated use weakens ice, so watch for cracks forming.

Overflow

Unfortunately for both the overland traveller and the bush pilot using a river or lake as a landing strip, the ice cover could have a layer of slushy water lying on its surface (overflow) that is hidden from view by the snow cover. This is a situation where the original cover of good (blue) ice on a lake has been inundated by water, which depending on the air temperature and the depth of snow lying atop the ice will remain as slush, freeze solid (white ice), or attain its own independent ice cover, in which case you will encounter layers of ice with water in between.

Most overflow conditions are caused by the weight of the snow cover or by a release of groundwater due to temperature change. The former depresses the ice surface below the hydrostatic water level to force water through cracks that have been created by the expansion and contraction of the ice as it responds to temperature change. In the

TABLE 2 — Critical Velocities for Moving Loads on Lake Ice

Water Depth		Critical Velocity*	
metres	feet	km/h	mph
1.2	4	14	8
1.8	6	18	11
2.4	8	19	12
3.0	10	22	13
4.5	15	27	17
6.0	20	30	18
9.0	30	35	22

* It is safer to travel below these speeds.
Note: These values are approximate only. More precise values will depend on ice thickness. When using a vehicle on a frozen surface, it is valuable to know that certain speeds (critical velocities) will create a hydrodynamic wave that will eventually result in ice-cover failure. The speed of the hydrodynamic wave depends on depth of water, thickness of cover, and degree of ice elasticity. If the vehicle speed coincides with that of the hydrodynamic wave, the stress on the cover due to the wave reinforces the stress that is due to the vehicle and can increase the maximum stress on the ice to the point of failure. Shallow water imposes more severe stress on the cover due to reflection of the wave from the bed. This table indicates critical velocities for moving loads on lake ice over shallow waters. It is safest to travel below these speeds. When approaching a lake shoreline or riverbank with ice thicknesses less than 75 centimetres (30 inches) your speed should not exceed 10 km/h (6 mph), and your angle of approach should be not less than 45 degrees. Considering static loads, the ice cover will sag continuously. The bearing capacity should be considered as 50% less than that for moving loads.

spring, groundwater release and the melt of the snow cover may also be responsible for an overflow condition.

Overflow is anathema to pilots of ski planes who may have landed on a lake or river of good black ice one day, only to experience frustration a month later when one or both skis encounter water beneath the snow cover, or break through a thin layer of frozen overflow into 15 centimetres (6 inches) of water lying atop the real (original) cover. The same conditions are a hazard to snowmobile operators and an annoyance to skiers and snowshoers. Sometimes only a part of a lake will have overflow. This condition is usually related to wind, which can blow snow from one part of the lake to another so that a localized heavy snow load will depress the ice cover at that location and not elsewhere.

Potentially Dangerous Areas

Most rivers and lakes north of 50 degrees latitude support a solid ice cover that can be used with caution as a natural highway or trail, from some time in early December to the end of April. There are, however, certain rivers (or certain reaches of them) in even higher latitudes that, for one reason or another, remain dangerous for the traveller to negotiate. It is not uncommon for rivers to remain open (completely ice-free) throughout the entire winter from the outlet of a lake to a point several miles downstream (a polynya). This is due to the deeper, warmer lake water rising to emerge at the usually shallow outlet where it can run free until it is cooled enough to freeze. For the same reason one may find open water, or very thin ice, at a shallow narrows separating two parts of a large lake. Like the lake outlet scenario there is likely to be an upwelling of warm water and a velocity, albeit slow, as water moves down the watershed.

At inlets of run-through lakes, the ice cover might be unsafe around the terminus of the river's delta, which is covered in ice. Such a region can usually be identified by the presence of a crusty and blotchy snow-ice surface. The danger lies in the fact that such sites can be one or two miles down-lake from the visible river mouth and surrounded by perfectly good (safe) ice. This is because there is a sharp drop-off at the terminus of the river delta so that the cold river water is constantly displacing the warmer lake water, which then rises to inhibit the growth of the lake's ice cover at that location.

ILLUSTRATION 1 — **Dangerous Locations on Frozen Rivers and Lakes**

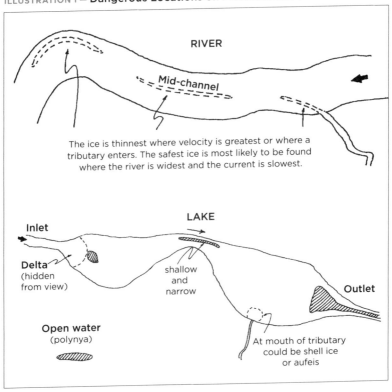

TO DO AND TO CARRY: TRAVEL PROCEDURES

If you plan to travel on ice, it is your responsibility to obtain as much local information as possible. Long-time residents of a particular region are usually aware of the ice calendar and, more importantly, specific danger areas (such as the deltas mentioned above). Whether you are travelling on skis, snowshoes, snowmobiles, or vehicles, you should adopt the following practices:

1. Travel in pairs whenever possible.

2. If you are the first to cross an ice cover, test ahead with a weighted prod while tethered to a companion who remains on shore. Do this without your pack and with your ski or

snowshoe harness undone (use shuffle gait). Have ice daggers (sometimes called icescapes) at the ready (usually suspended from a cord around the neck).

3. Carry tools that will allow you to measure ice thickness, but do so clear of the shoreline. Ice near the lakeshore or riverbank is rarely representative of the cover; 6 metres (20 feet) out from either the ice could be much thicker. Once you know the thickness you can then refer to the table that relates thickness to load-bearing capacity. Remember that river ice is weaker than lake ice.

4. Try to identify the type of ice by texture, colour, and the sound it makes when hit with your prod pole. (A hollow sound is a sign of a weaker shell ice.)

5. Remember that repeated use (passage) weakens ice.

6. Proceed in echelon, break rhythm, use a shuffle step, walk pigeon-toed, and keep moving. All these precautions—both taken individually and better yet in concert—can reduce the impact.

7. Always carry a length of light line (15 metres by 12 millimetres, 50 feet by ⅜ inch diameter) when you are travelling on foot. When travelling by snowmobile, make sure you have a tow rope.

8. If using a snowmobile, watch your speed. The hydrodynamic shock wave that may occur could have dire results (See Table 1).

9. Consider the practicality of carrying a light pole lashed across a snowmobile.

10. Know how to treat a victim of hypothermia.

When you are the first person to use a specific route shortly after freeze-up, proceed with extra caution. Even if you have taken the same path in the past, this is no guarantee of safe passage. The formation of ice, due to date and temperature differences, is not likely to be the same from one winter to the next. You could be pioneering a new route at any time.

Ice Tools

There are numerous available hand and motorized tools that can be used for making a hole in an ice cover to measure its thickness, or simply to obtain water, permit ice fishing, or allow the entry of a diver. To make a hole manually requires effort no matter what tool is used. Trappers occupying line cabins will likely go to the nearest creek, river, or lake with an axe. A few whacks, and there will be enough chips of ice for cooking and washing. Ice fishers will benefit from something a shade more efficient than an axe, especially if the ice is thick.

A person limited to manual tools will, in all probability, use a needle bar, an ice chisel, or a Swedish ice auger. If using mechanized transport and needs to drill many holes through the ice, they will use one of the many motorized ice augers that are currently available.

Those who live beyond the range of municipal utilities such as water and sewer systems, or those who have no well, must haul water from the nearest source. For many, this could mean keeping a water hole open in the ice throughout the winter. To save work, once a hole in the ice is cut large enough to accept a bucket or dipper, it is common practice to cover it with some sort of insulation. By so doing only a skim of surface ice will have to be removed the following day. Some northern residents cut out blocks of ice with an ice saw, which can then be hauled on a sled to a large container inside the house. Apart from the acquisition of water for domestic use, scientists may use an ice saw to cut a very large hole in the ice for the purpose of providing an entry point for divers, large instruments, or robot submersibles.

While still on the subject of hand tools, it should be mentioned that to be effective the cutting edge of any tool used to cut ice must be absolutely razor sharp. I have mentioned the Swedish ice drill, which works reasonably well in good lake ice that has few impurities in it and is of moderate thickness. The same drill is almost useless on river ice, where stones or sand are likely to be in suspension and will immediately dull the blade.

Mini Ice Drill

For the purpose of measuring ice thickness to determine bearing strength for safe travel purposes, or for obtaining drinking water, a timber-boring bit (or ship's auger) of 1.5 centimetres (⅝ inch) diameter can be used with a carpenter's brace (see Illustration 2). To adapt such a bit for ice, grind off the leader-screw at the tip. Such a drill bit is lightweight and compact but can only be used for ice thicknesses not exceeding 40 centimetres (18 inches), which is usually the longest bit available at any hardware store.

If you are using such a tool simply to obtain water, first cut a shallow depression in the ice with an axe and bore the hole at the lowest point. This will allow the use of a dipper when the depression fills with water. A short graduated stick with a protruding screw at one end to hook under the ice cover can be used to determine thickness.

Ice Prod and Makeshift Chisel

The traveller on skis or snowshoes will certainly have no desire to pack a proper (heavy) ice chisel to test the cover of any lake or river he or she may wish to cross. But what we can carry in our pack is an attachment to our ski pole (or any pole cut from the bush) that will give us a suitable ice prod. If the head of this attachment is shaped appropriately it can also be used as a makeshift chisel to access water through a thin ice cover. A light ski pole by itself may not penetrate unsafe ice, but if a steel point of a reasonable weight can be readily attached and it breaks through, then the cover is not safe to traverse.

ILLUSTRATION 2 — **A Handy Ice Tool**

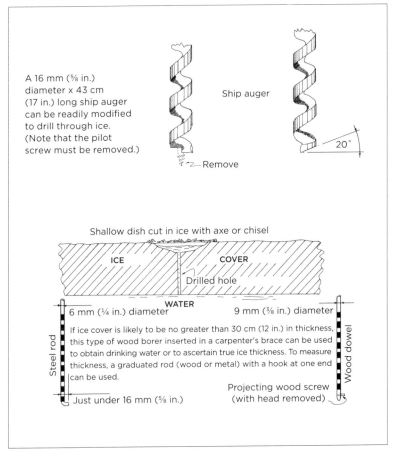

A 16 mm (⅝ in.) diameter x 43 cm (17 in.) long ship auger can be readily modified to drill through ice. (Note that the pilot screw must be removed.)

Ship auger

20°

Remove

Shallow dish cut in ice with axe or chisel

ICE

COVER

Drilled hole

WATER

6 mm (¼ in.) diameter

9 mm (⅜ in.) diameter

Steel rod

If ice cover is likely to be no greater than 30 cm (12 in.) in thickness, this type of wood borer inserted in a carpenter's brace can be used to obtain drinking water or to ascertain true ice thickness. To measure thickness, a graduated rod (wood or metal) with a hook at one end can be used.

Just under 16 mm (⅝ in.)

Wood dowel

Projecting wood screw (with head removed)

The hose clamps used to secure this item to the pole are handy to have in one's travel kit (especially useful for any splicing). This chisel-pointed attachment can be made using a 1.3-centimetre- (½-inch-) diameter by 30.5-centimetre- (12-inch-) long lag screw obtainable at most hardware stores. The head of the screw is cut to form the chisel. Two 3.8-centimetre (1.5-inch) hose clamps will permit its attachment to either end of a ski pole (or any pole). In addition to its use as a probe, the chisel configuration will allow the chipping of a small hole to access water for consumption.

ILLUSTRATION 3 — **Ski-Pole Ice Chisel and Prod**

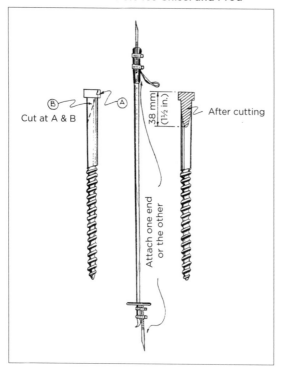

Cut at A & B

After cutting

38 mm (1½ in.)

Attach one end or the other

Ice Dagger

This device, which helps one climb onto a slippery ice surface after being unexpectedly immersed, may be referred to by many different names, but I have chosen to refer to it as ice dagger. It is not a common item of equipment, but it should be. It is very difficult to regain the surface of an ice cover if you have become fully immersed and your clothing has had time to become saturated. To break through thin ice while on foot or driving a dog team, snowmobile, or truck is not as uncommon an event as one would imagine, especially in the periods (shortly after freeze-up and before breakup) when people are anxious to get going or to extend their use of the cover. Using daggers and kicking with your feet will help you climb onto the ice surface. But the best option is having someone close by with a rescue line.

ILLUSTRATION 4 — **Ice Dagger**

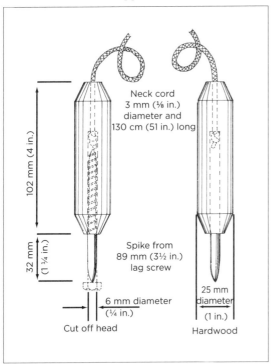

Neck cord
3 mm (⅛ in.)
diameter and
130 cm (51 in.) long

102 mm (4 in.)

32 mm (1 ¼ in.)

Spike from
89 mm (3½ in.)
lag screw

6 mm diameter
(¼ in.)

Cut off head

25 mm
diameter
(1 in.)

Hardwood

A Canadian Red Cross report from 2006 says that from 1991 to 2000 there were 447 deaths in Canada associated with activities on ice. Of these, 246 involved people on snowmobiles, 150 were non-motorized, and 51 were motorized. Most of these numbers related to recreational activities. What is regrettable is that most of these accidents could have been easily avoided had those involved had some knowledge of ice characteristics, rescue techniques, and equipment that would facilitate a rescue process.

There are many precautions we can take when crossing frozen bodies of water, as outlined elsewhere in this book. I cannot, however, overemphasize the importance of the ice dagger. This convenient and easy-to-carry piece of equipment could be vital, especially if you are alone. Ice daggers are common in Scandinavian countries and why they are not regarded as essential equipment in North America is hard to explain. It is an item that anyone can make. All you need is two short and sturdy screwdrivers filed, or ground, to a point (see Illustration 4). Carry your ice dagger on a neck cord and protect the points with a common sheath such as a short piece of wood with a hole bored at each end to take the spike. It could save your life!

Ice Chisel

Before making any reference to motorized equipment I would like to elaborate a little on the most-loved of all tools: the ice chisel. A properly designed chisel is the best tool for cutting a hole in ice by hand. A good ice chisel will allow the penetration of thick ice in the most efficient way. When a person can cut a 30-centimetre (12-inch) by 60-centimetre (24-inch) hole through 122 centimetres (48 inches) in 15 to 20 minutes using this tool, we have sufficient proof of its effectiveness (the dimensions quoted permit the use of a snow shovel to facilitate chip removal). The essential factor to allow such efficiency is the design of the chisel.

Illustration 5 gives dimensions and details of what I consider a useful chisel. Such a chisel may also be used as a prod to test for safe ice. The shaft of the chisel is made of wood, which is more comfortable to hold in cold temperatures and is of large enough diameter that it may be gripped by a mitt-encased hand with no fear of cramping. Chisels with smaller diameters are difficult to hold for any length of time and have a tendency to shatter upon impact. Ideally, a timber-framing chisel, or commercial carpenter's slick (a very large chisel), is used for the blade; these have just the right temper. It should be noted that the bevel of the cutting edge should extend back at least 2.5 centimetres (1 inch) to allow good penetration at every blow. If such blades are not procurable, the alternative is to use a piece of truck spring, which is welded to the steel tubing that provides the chisel's weight and accommodates the wooden shaft.

To achieve the correct point of balance, cut the steel tubing to an appropriate length. I would suggest starting with a piece 41 centimetres

(16 inches) in length. The back of the blade should be in line with the outside dimension of the tubing. The "Dee" handle is always oriented in the same plane as the chisel blade. The total weight of this short version should be 4.5 kilograms (10 pounds).

Chopping ice is like tree-felling or log-cutting; you have to have the right tool and it has to be sharp. Because river ice is often impregnated with sand or even rocks, you must keep a file handy. The other important factor is, of course, technique. The essential thing to remember is that high impact contributes to good penetration and the shattering of ice; you will get nowhere pecking at it. In order to get a good force behind every stroke without straining your back, you must keep the chisel as close to your body as possible. There can be no real force given to the chisel with your arm extended in a cantilever fashion. The basic technique demands that the chisel be angled very slightly toward the centre of the hole with

ILLUSTRATION 5 — **Yukon (Short) Ice Chisel**

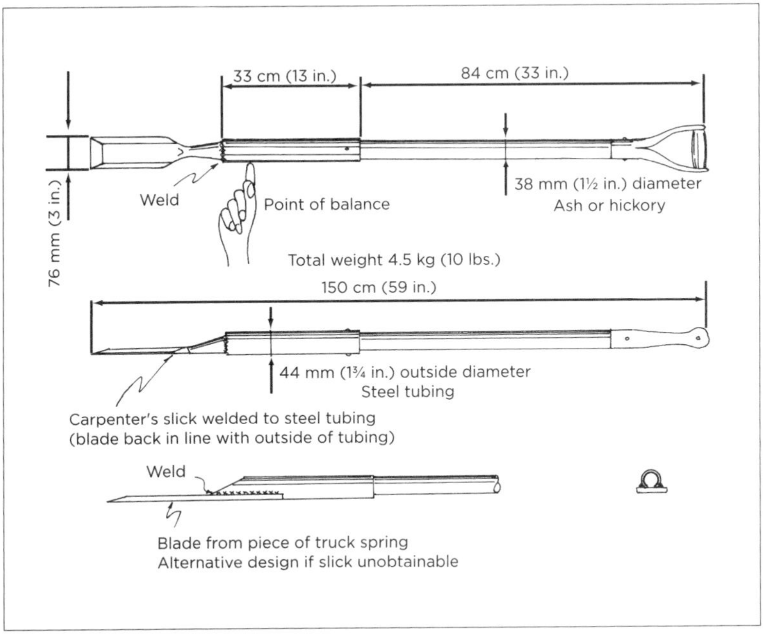

33 cm (13 in.)

84 cm (33 in.)

76 mm (3 in.)

Weld   Point of balance

38 mm (1½ in.) diameter
Ash or hickory

Total weight 4.5 kg (10 lbs.)

150 cm (59 in.)

44 mm (1¾ in.) outside diameter
Steel tubing

Carpenter's slick welded to steel tubing
(blade back in line with outside of tubing)

Weld

Blade from piece of truck spring
Alternative design if slick unobtainable

ILLUSTRATION 6 — **Ice-Chiselling Technique**

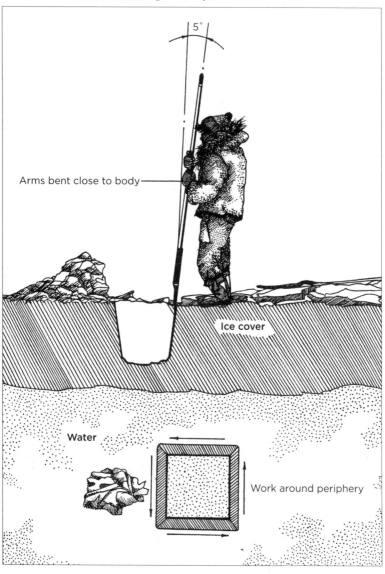

5°

Arms bent close to body

Ice cover

Water

Work around periphery

the bevel of the blade facing inward. The chiseller merely follows the periphery of his hole until break through is accomplished. There is never any need to touch the centre of the hole with the chisel; the ice will shatter by itself.

A word of warning: keep a firm hold on the chisel when you are near breakthrough (detected by a distinct hollow sound). It is easy to lose your grip and say goodbye to a good tool. Tying a cord (lanyard) to the chisel and securing the free end to either your wrist or waist is a good idea.

Needle Bar

An alternative to the ice chisel is the all-steel needle bar (see Illustration 7), sworn by many to be a superb tool. Many northern residents have relied upon a pointed steel rod for their water supply and for penetrating ice for the purpose of setting fishnets.

The needle bar is a single-component tool formed from a steel rod about 2 centimetres (¾ inches) diameter. The lower part is forged into a triangular cross-section that is brought to a long taper, ending in a needle point.

The efficiency of this tool stems from the fact that the needle point will shatter ice on impact. It does this very well. The weakness of the needle bar is that it is cold to handle, has too small a shaft for sustained use, and produces a jagged hole that is not easy to clear of chips if the ice is thick. This will not be such a disadvantage to anyone who merely wishes to obtain a water supply.

ILLUSTRATION 7 —

Needle Bar

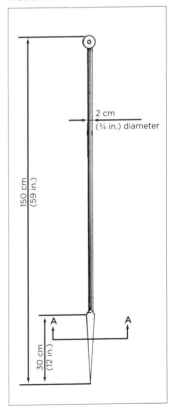

2 cm (¾ in.) diameter

150 cm (59 in.)

30 cm (12 in.)

A

A

Swedish Ice Drill

This popular hand tool consists of a hand crank, a shaft, and a spoon-shaped blade (cutter) with the inside edge beveled to provide a suitable cutting angle (see Illustration 8). An alternative design utilizes two replaceable cutting blades attached to a length of flighting. In both instances the corkscrew-like flighting removes the cuttings from the hole as the assembly rotates.

This type of hand drill can be useful for the penetration of lake ice that is absolutely clean and not too thick. It is invariably useless for drilling through river ice, which is most likely impregnated with sand, small stones, or even boulders. The blade, or blades, must be kept razor sharp at all times, and it is advisable to carry a supply of these so that quick changes can be affected in the field. Some Swedish ice drills have a folding handle, so they are not only lightweight but also very compact.

ILLUSTRATION 8 — **Hand Ice Drills**

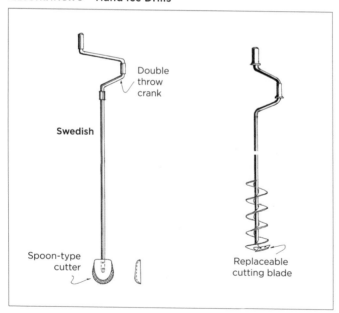

Motorized Ice Drills

There is a wide range of motorized ice equipment on the market today. Most serious ice fishermen rely on motorized ice augers. Some motorized ice drills are simply chainsaws that have been converted by adding a gearbox or, as it is more descriptively called, a drilling attachment. Other models consist of a two-stroke motor specifically designed to power a gearbox, which accommodates the flighting and a removable drill bit.

Bits and flighting come in various sizes, so that holes from 10 to 25 centimetres (4 to 10 inches) in diameter can be drilled quickly through thick ice. Various lengths of flighting can be bolted together to allow drilling through very thick ice. To penetrate the sea ice of the Beaufort Sea, for example, you will require at least 4 metres (13 feet) of flighting.

The drill bits in common use are designed either to shave the ice, like a wood bit, or to scarify it as a serrated grader blade scrapes an ice-covered highway. For shaving purposes, the blades are straight-edged. For scarifying, they have a multi-toothed cutting edge. Whatever type of bit is used, it must be of such a hardness to allow sharpening with a file in the field. For efficient cutting, the critical parts of the bit include the outer tip and the centre cutter (lead), which is often removable. This does not mean, however, that you shouldn't have a spare bit or two in your day pack.

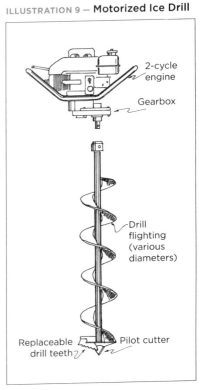

ILLUSTRATION 9 — **Motorized Ice Drill**

2-cycle engine

Gearbox

Drill flighting (various diameters)

Replaceable drill teeth

Pilot cutter

Chainsaw

An alternative to the mechanized ice drill is the good old chainsaw. Possible disadvantages of this instrument for ice cutting include damage to the chain through contact with sand or stones imbedded in the ice (mostly a problem on rivers). It is also messier at the time of breakthrough since water will be thrown up to freeze on your clothes and will accumulate on the saw itself, especially in very cold temperatures. Another disadvantage is the difficulty of ice-block removal, especially if the ice is thick.

Swedish Ice Saw

Although it is rarely seen today, the Swedish ice saw is a handy tool for anyone wishing to lay up blocks of ice or to cut a large opening in an ice cover. The saw depicted in Illustration 10 is made of stainless steel of a thickness a little more than a carpenter's saw. The teeth (often 46 in number for such a length) are 38 millimetres (1.5 inches) in depth, dressed on alternate sides and given a set of 4 millimetres ($^5/_{32}$ inch). A long, round, wooden handle is placed through the holes in the metal handle.

ILLUSTRATION 10 — **Swedish Ice Saw**

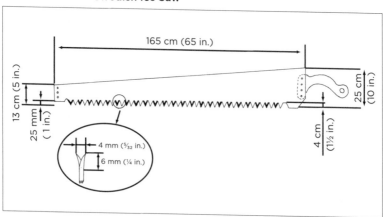

A traveller on skis follows a dog team trail on the left bank of the Yukon River near the mouth of the White River.

chapter 3

~

SNOW

OF ALL THE FORMS of precipitation, snow is the most beautiful and inspiring. Many traditions associated with Christmas call for a nivean landscape. Poems and songs have immortalized the snowflake. Its six-pointed symbol has traditionally been used for decoration and as the basic design of many insignia including that of the Order of Canada.

Snowflakes fall as one or more ice crystals. To put it in simplified terms, crystals form when water vapour freezes around a particle that serves as a nucleating agent, often a dust particle. Crystals appear in many different forms—needles, plates, or hollow hexagonal columns, depending on the air temperature and available vapour supply during the formation process. In reality, snow formation is a very complex process—so complex that there is an International Snow Classification System that categorizes ten types of falling precipitation: plate, stellar crystal, column, needle, spatial dendrite, capped column, irregular crystal, graupel, ice pellet, and hail.

Animals have adapted to a land of snow and ice by developing physical features that facilitate ease of travel either over the surface of snow or through it. For example, hares, lynxes, foxes, and wolves travel on top of snow, whereas moose travel through it. Caribou, with hooves that give support, are chionophiles. They range south of their summer (tundra) grazing grounds to the treeline, where the softer snow can be readily pawed through for feed. Russian scientists have coined specific words to classify fauna in relation to their behaviour in snow. Chioneuphores are those that have adjusted to living through winter. Chionophiles have specific features that allow them to live in a northern winter. Chionophobes are animals that are unable to adjust to snow conditions.

Snow cover provides insulation to several small creatures that inhabit a subnivean environment, which is much warmer than the ambient air temperature. It is in this *pukak* layer that mice, voles, shrews, lemmings, and squirrels scurry through a labyrinth of tunnels where the temperature is rarely colder than 0°C to −10°C regardless of the air temperature at the surface. Not only are these creatures protected from the extremes of cold but also from surface and airborne predators. Grouse and ptarmigan often take advantage of the insulating quality of the snow blanket by plunging into snowdrifts at night.

Caribou—a true chionophile in the Richardson Mountains.

Because of the dominance and importance of snow in the life of those who must hunt and travel in winter, and because there are so many different types of snow, it has a lexicon all its own (see Appendix B).

TRAVEL ON SNOW

People of northern indigenous cultures have responded in many different ways to the challenge of mobility over snow. To facilitate overland travel, they use various types of snowshoes—from small ones with course-meshed webbing for a dense snow cover to long, wider ones with fine-meshed webbing and turned-up tips for a thick cover of light snow. The Inuit are able to walk without snowshoes on the harder wind-packed snow of the tundra and the polar sea. Northern First Nations people use toboggans on the soft snow of the forest while Inuit have traditionally used a type of sleds called a *kamotik*, which has narrow runners that run well on a hard snow or ice surface.

Snowshoes

A trapper pauses at a pressure ridge on Atlin Lake with snowshoes that show the traditional First Nations rawhide hitch.

ILLUSTRATION 12 — **A Traditional First Nations Snowshoe Hitch**

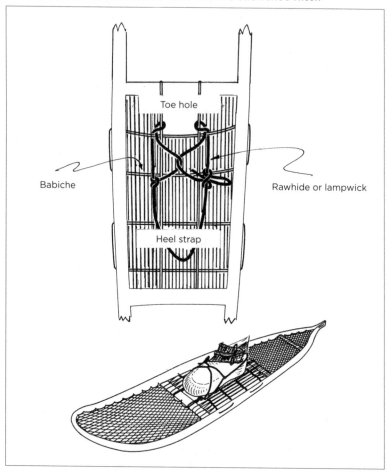

Toe hole

Babiche

Rawhide or lampwick

Heel strap

Originating in North America, snowshoes have long been essential for the winter traveller. Since early times, various designs of these tennis racquet–like frameworks have prevented the wearer from sinking into deep snow, making it possible to travel over a wide variety of snow conditions and almost all types of terrain.

Snowshoes make it possible to weave a path through thick forest and the deepest snow with little handicap. Unlike skis, no special skill or footwear is required. If you wear moccasins, or mukluks, you may use a harness made from strips of moose or caribou hide tied to form a "First Nations hitch" (see page 46) into which you can twist your foot. After the appearance of the Caucasian trader, the same hitches were made using lampwick instead of rawhide. There is no need to touch the snowshoe, no knots to tie, no straps or buckles to secure—a great convenience, especially in sub-zero temperatures when hands are mitt-encased and should stay that way.

Traditionally, snowshoe frames were made of white ash or birch with rawhide webs and bindings. Many present-day manufacturers of snowshoes still use wood and untanned cowhide, while others have taken advantage of more modern materials. More common today is light alloy tubing for the frame and neoprene or Hypalon for the web to make a lighter, stronger snowshoe with greater resistance to wetting and wear. Though lacking the warm aesthetic charm of wood, some of the best snowshoes today are made of these materials.

The military have for some time used a magnesium frame model with a web made of coated aircraft cable. (I suspect that titanium frames are just around the corner, with some exotic material being used for the web). Nowadays many snowshoes have a solid deck rather than cross-lacing, though the latter offers a better grip on the snow. Purists (some might call them romantics) stick with the aesthetically beautiful ash or birch. Wooden snowshoes serve well with annual maintenance (especially necessary if the shoes have been used in wet snow). Yearly coatings of Varathane will help frames and rawhide webs last for many winters. Be extremely wary of any snowshoe moulded of plastic, despite the claims made by the maker.

Snowshoes (see page 49) can be used in extreme cold because the various harnesses can be adjusted to accommodate all manner of footwear, including the bulky polar boot. Just make sure that the toe hole is large enough to accommodate this type of boot.

Snowshoe Travel

The many different shapes and sizes of snowshoes we see today do not reflect, as I once thought, the artistic whim of the maker. The reasons for variation are more objective than that. Certain design features, including shapes and sizes, lend themselves either to specific snow conditions, different types of terrain, or for specific uses such as mountaineering. Some shapes will allow you to use the forepart of the frame as a shovel when constructing a snow shelter.

Snowshoe Tips

Select snowshoes that are as small and lightweight as possible, giving appropriate consideration to the weight they will have to support (body weight plus clothing plus day pack), the terrain you intend to negotiate, and predominant snow conditions in your area.

A long snowshoe with a high turned-up toe is well suited to deep, loose snow.

The best snowshoes for climbing are those with bindings located far forward and with a turn-up of about 11 centimetres (4 to 5 inches). To satisfy the needs of mountaineers, several snowshoe designs include a traction device, which is integral to the harness. A hinged claw serves like a crampon to offer a good grip on steep slopes. (In the old days this need was served by wrapping pieces of rope along the sides of the frame to form a rough edge that, being at right angles to the direction of travel, would bite into the snow and, being soft, would reduce slippage on ice.)

The best snowshoe for hillside use is 20 to 23 centimetres (8 to 9 inches) wide.

A person on snowshoes can break a good trail for a toboggan, sled, or dog team.

Some travellers (myself included) like to use ski poles when snowshoeing. Ski poles can be of great help in hill country and can also be used as prods to detect unsupported snow cover, as tent anchors, or as part of a roof over a snow trench emergency shelter.

Round-toed snowshoes can be used as makeshift snow shovels.

TABLE 3 — Snowshoes

TYPE	ADVANTAGES	DISADVANTAGES
Bearpaw	Best on gentle terrain with deep, soft snow; easy to manoeuvre; round tails offer good floatation.	Somewhat awkward; unless binding is well forward, they will not track well; wider models unsuited to mountain travel.
Modified Bearpaw	Tracks better than true bearpaw; suitable for both forest and mountain travel; best on firm snow.	Not ideal for descending; the rear webbing tends to wear on all bearpaw shoes.
Beavertail	Good tracking; suited to mountain and forest travel provided it has good front turn-up and width does not exceed 30 centimetres (12 inches).	Usual width a disadvantage on sidehills and when descending.
Yudon Trailer (Alaska Trapper)	Good for plunge-stepping downhill; good on flats in deep powder; excellent tracking.	Not quite as convenient as other models to handle in forests.
Ojibway	Versatile model; turned-up toes break crust on lift step; similar to the "Teslin" shoe favoured by Yukoners; good for mountain and forest travel.	Cannot be used as a shovel for building a snowhouse.

Skis

While skis have been used for travel in Scandinavian countries for hundreds of years it is only in recent times that cross-country skiing and ski-touring have become popular in North America.

The advantage of skis over snowshoes is obvious. On the level—crossing lakes, plateaus, and glaciers—or where there is a packed surface, skis will allow a much faster rate of travel because you glide a little at every stride. The other advantage is that you can develop a less-tiring rhythm, which is not always possible using snowshoes. If climbing, you can attach skins to your skis, and

TABLE 4 — **Rates of Travel on Foot, Snowshoes, and Skis**

TYPE OF TRAVEL	RATE OF TRAVEL	
	km/h	mph
Walking without pack over good, mostly level, open ground wearing hiking boots	5-6	3-4
Walking over hilly terrain with day pack	3-4	2-2.5
Walking through forest with need to avoid trees (not dense undergrowth); no trail	2-3	1.5-2
Walking on snowshoes that sink no more than 5 centimetres (2 inches); open ground	4-5	2.5-3
Breaking trail on snowshoes sinking 25 centimetres (10 inches); open ground	2-2.5	1-1.5
Breaking trail on snowshoes sinking 30 centimetres (12 inches) or more	1	0.75
Breaking trail on snowshoes, carrying pack and sinking more than 31 centimetres (12 inches)	0.5-1	0.5
Travelling on cross-country skis on packed trail, level terrain, no pack	8-11	5-7
Travelling on cross-country skis on packed trail, level terrain, with 18-kilogram (40-pound) pack	5-6	3-4

Note: If you are pulling a small sled, your rate of travel will be close to that quoted for a person toting an 18-kilogram (40-pound) pack. Figures are based on a six-hour day. With longer days of travel, the values drop dramatically.

every downhill section can usually be negotiated with considerable speed.

On the downside the use of skis demands some expertise and technique. The ski-tourer will be seriously handicapped traversing deep snow on level terrain and where the route passes through brush or dense forest. The trail made by a skier on virgin snow does not make a good path for a sled.

Anyone travelling in an environment of intense cold will find that skis do not glide well on very cold snow. Make sure you select a ski boot that provides adequate cold-weather protection.

For maximum versatility, the winter traveller doing an overland journey involving all kinds of terrain and snow conditions should consider carrying both skis and snowshoes. If you are forced to remove your skis or snowshoes to cross glare ice on foot, it is also nice to have a pair of lightweight **ice-creepers** (studded plates that can be strapped to your footwear). When the wind is favourable, some skiers use kites to increase their speed when crossing lakes or plateaus. Whatever ski or snowshoe equipment you use, it is important to carry a mini tool kit to fix breakages as well as spare ski tips and harness parts. It is also useful to carry something that could be used to splice a ski pole, like a hose clamp. Stainless steel wire is another important item to have in your repair kit.

Sleds

The origin of the sled is unknown, though there is evidence that sleds were used in the Neolithic period, and certainly the Inuit were using them many thousands of years ago. Historical references to sleds are not so surprising when you consider that while you may pack 18 kilogram (40 pounds) without too much discomfort, it is possible to pull three times that weight on a sled that offers little frictional resistance with little distress.

The first sleds were probably animal hides pulled fur-side-down with the lay of the fur. There are references to sled runners being made from wetted, rolled-up skins that were allowed to freeze shaped in the form of a runner. Sled runners have been contrived from whalebone and driftwood. Later, timber runners were shod with mud frozen in place, then coated with water (or spit), which froze to provide a surface offering minimal resistance. Nowadays, the runners of sleds and boards of toboggans are shod with a hard plastic that is not only resistant to wear but that also provides a good sliding surface.

Many species of animals have been used to haul sleds, sleighs, or sledges. Reindeer, horses, goats, and dogs have all been used as traction animals. Polar explorers from many countries have made the most amazing journeys either using dogs to pull their sleds or simply, but most arduously, by man-hauling. When conditions allow, square sails (often a tent groundsheet) have been erected on sleds to make faster progress across lakes or plateaus.

Types of Sleds

Nansen sled—The foremost improvement in sled design was the frame-type sled designed by notable Norwegian polar explorer Fridtjof Nansen to make the first crossing of Greenland in 1888. Nansen used this sled in 1895 for the epic journey from his ship the *Fram* (at that time frozen in the ice pack at latitude 84 degrees north) to latitude 86 degrees, 15 minutes, and thence to near Franz Josef Land, where he was picked up, quite unexpectedly, by members of a British expedition. This type of sled was also used by Roald Amundsen to reach the South Pole in 1912 and by such other well-known polar explorers as Robert Falcon Scott, Ernest Shackleton, and Douglas Mawson.

It is basically a light framework built on a pair of long skis with all joints lashed with strips of rawhide to make it flexible; it is best suited to ice-cap travel or open terrain.

Kamotik—Also called *komotik, kamut,* or *komatik,* reflecting the many dialects spoken across the polar North. This is the traditional Inuit sled, made to withstand the rough surface of the frozen polar sea. It is constructed of a hefty pair of solid runners joined together by numerous plank-like cross members. Like on the Nansen sled, all members are lashed together to provide the flexibility essential for durability. The *kamotik* does not have handlebars (a feature on Nansen and Greenland sleds).

Greenland sled—This type of sled is structurally similar to the *kamotik* because it runs on the lower edges of two solid sides and is decked with board lashed, or wedged, to the sides. Unlike the *kamotik,* it has handlebars and is shorter in length.

ILLUSTRATION 13 — **Nansen Sled**

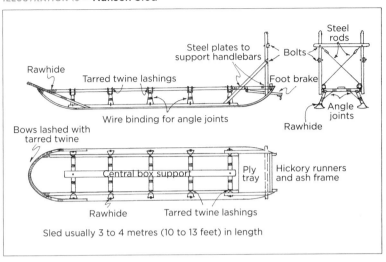

Steel plates to support handlebars
Bolts
Steel rods
Rawhide
Tarred twine lashings
Foot brake
Angle joints
Wire binding for angle joints
Rawhide
Bows lashed with tarred twine
Central box support
Ply tray
Hickory runners and ash frame
Rawhide
Tarred twine lashings
Sled usually 3 to 4 metres (10 to 13 feet) in length

ILLUSTRATION 14 — **Greenland Sled**

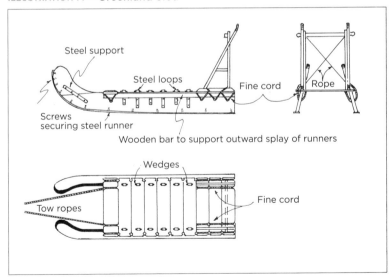

Steel support
Steel loops
Fine cord
Rope
Screws securing steel runner
Wooden bar to support outward splay of runners
Wedges
Tow ropes
Fine cord

ILLUSTRATION 15 — **Kamotik (Kamut)**

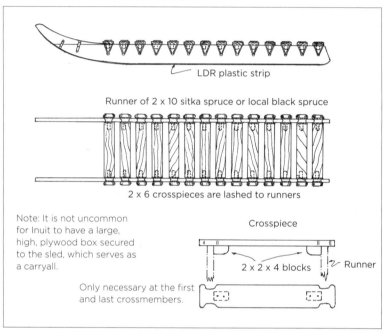

LDR plastic strip

Runner of 2 x 10 sitka spruce or local black spruce

2 x 6 crosspieces are lashed to runners

Note: It is not uncommon for Inuit to have a large, high, plywood box secured to the sled, which serves as a carryall.

Crosspiece

2 x 2 x 4 blocks

Runner

Only necessary at the first and last crossmembers.

Kamotik sled production at Nain, Labrador.

Toboggan — While the Inuit used sleds to travel over open terrain, the indigenous people of the forest, where deep, soft snow is endemic, have used birch toboggans anywhere from 25 to 40 centimetres (10 to 16 inches) in width, which is the size of a track made by a person on snowshoes. With high turned-up bows and lengths that varied from 3 to 6 metres (10 to 20 feet), such toboggans offered a good bearing surface and were quite flexible.

Pulka — Lightweight and sturdy, of Lapp origin, this is another type of sled–toboggan composite. Nowadays made of moulded plastic, fibreglass or magnesium alloy, pulkas are very popular with ski-tourers, surveyors, mountaineers, foresters, military, and search-and-rescue personnel.

Disposable sled — You can make a very cheap, and therefore, disposable, alternative to the fibreglass pulka by attaching a harness of plastic tubing to a child's plastic sled. This is good for someone making a one-shot journey.

Portable open-terrain sled — This is a sled that I have found most useful in the course of my working life as a hydrometric surveyor. It can be carried in an assembled form lashed to an internal frame pack used to carry your pack or quickly dismantled for stowage in a light aircraft or helicopter (see photos on pages 59–60).

ILLUSTRATION 16 — **Work sled**

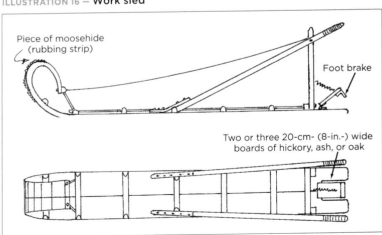

ILLUSTRATION 17 — Work toboggan

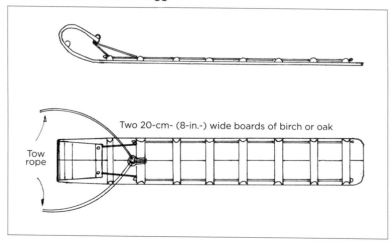

Two 20-cm- (8-in.-) wide boards of birch or oak

Tow rope

ILLUSTRATION 18 — Fibreglass Pulka

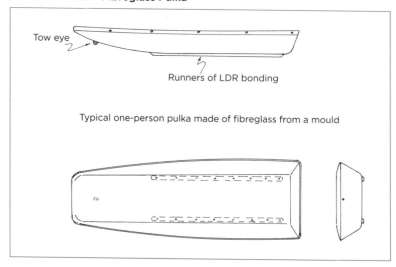

Tow eye

Runners of LDR bonding

Typical one-person pulka made of fibreglass from a mould

ILLUSTRATION 19 — **Older-type Combination Sled-Toboggan**

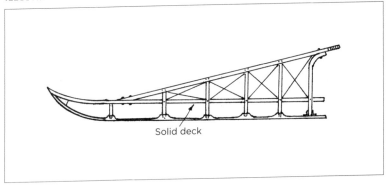

Solid deck

ILLUSTRATION 20 — **Disposable Pulka (good for mountain traverse)**

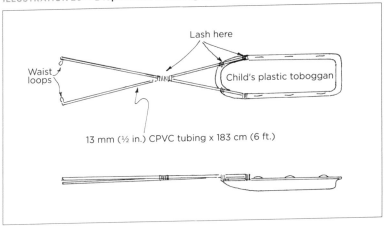

Lash here

Waist loops

Child's plastic toboggan

13 mm (½ in.) CPVC tubing x 183 cm (6 ft.)

ILLUSTRATION 21 AND 22 — **Portable Open-Terrain Sled**

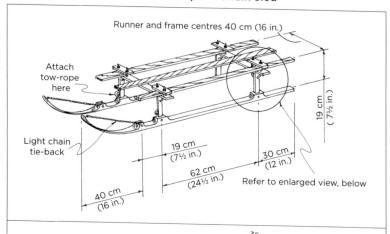

Runner and frame centres 40 cm (16 in.)

Attach
tow-rope
here

19 cm
(7½ in.)

Light chain
tie-back

19 cm
(7½ in.)

30 cm
(12 in.)

62 cm
(24½ in.)

Refer to enlarged view, below

40 cm
(16 in.)

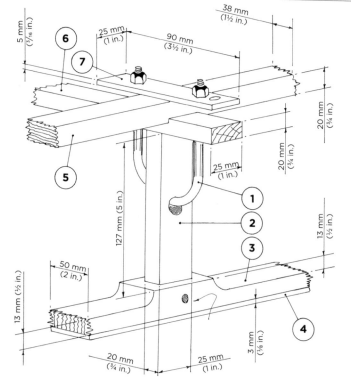

5 mm
(³/₁₆ in.)

38 mm
(1½ in.)

6

25 mm
(1 in.)

90 mm
(3½ in.)

7

20 mm
(¾ in.)

5

20 mm
(¾ in.)

127 mm (5 in.)

25 mm
(1 in.)

1

2

13 mm (½ in.)

13 mm (½ in.)

3

50 mm
(2 in.)

4

3 mm (⅛ in.)

20 mm
(¾ in.)

25 mm
(1 in.)

1. 5 cm (2 in.) "U" bolt (key part of sled)   **2.** Leg of hardwood   **3.** Sled runner
of oak or ash   **4.** Running strip of hard plastic   **5.** Longitudinal member of
oak   **6.** Crossmember of oak   **7.** Clamp plate of light alloy

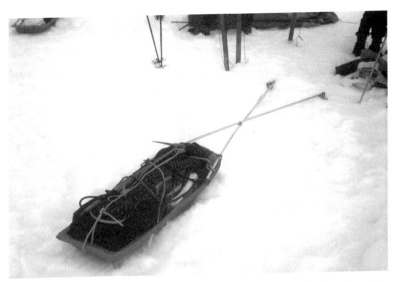

A loaded sled of the disposable type.

Portable open-terrain sled carrying an expedition pack.

Portable open-terrain sled being carried on an expedition pack with a fibreglass pulka in the foreground.

Open-terrain sled on Lake Bennett on the BC–Yukon border.

Using Sleds

Before loading any sled or toboggan, cover the base with a large enough piece of light canvas so that the load can be encased prior to lashing. If you are man-hauling, you have the choice of a rigid harness, which affords good control over the sled, or a simple tow (trace) line. The harness has a distinct advantage when you are crossing hilly terrain, whereas the tow line can be used to some advantage when traversing flat country or lakes. You can use a bungee cord with the tow line to absorb the jerky movement that occurs when crossing a generally flat but uneven surface.

When traversing flat terrain, especially with a hard surface, I have found that two light pulka-type sleds are easier to pull than a single heavy one. This also gives the advantage of having loads that are shorter in height, not only to make the sled more stable but also to make equipment more accessible. Two light sleds can often be lifted over obstacles (such as pressure ridges on lakes) in a loaded state.

The best sleds for snowmobilers are the frame (Nansen) type, various metal pulka-type designs, two- or three-board toboggans, and traditional Inuit sleds. No matter what type of sled is used, there should be a shock link (spring) between machine and sled. Emergency sleds have been made using skis as runners and ski poles as cross braces.

When crossing sea ice, lakes, glaciers, and polar plateaus with a sled, it is common practice to use a sail. A tent groundsheet can double as a square sail. A pair of skis can serve as the mast with ski poles as cross arms. As mentioned earlier, kites have also been used.

When crossing a crevassed glacier, it is prudent to lash a long pole atop the load and to trail a long line. Both devices have prevented sleds from disappearing into an abyss.

Special sleds have been made for polar-sea travel where **open leads** (channels in ice fields) pose a constant threat. Such sleds are double-hulled to offer flotation. In the early days of polar-sea travel, it was common practice for explorers to carry kayaks atop their sleds.

Two Nansen sleds, lashed side by side, can be covered with canvas to make a raft.

Sled Tie-Downs

All equipment has to be securely tied to the frame of the sled, toboggan, or pulka. Quite often a single long cord is used. Tied at the front of the sled, the cord is usually passed from one side of the sled to the other in diagonal loops to be finally secured at the rear, or carried criss-cross back to the front. Spaced lashing hooks, or side loops, running along the base of the sled facilitate this process. Sturdy bungee cords can be used to replace the lashing line or in concert with it.

Anyone using a line (whether it is a climbing rope or new synthetic cordage) will benefit from knowing at least three knots: one to make a loop and the other to join two lengths together. The knots that best satisfy such usage are the bowline and carrick bend.

ILLUSTRATION 23 — **Knots**

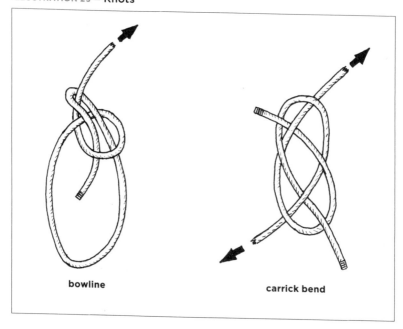

bowline   carrick bend

SNOW AS A SHELTER-BUILDING MATERIAL

One of the advantages of travel across snow-covered terrain is that building material is readily available. Some travellers choose to leave their tents at home, relying entirely on their ability to construct a shelter of snow at the end of each day. In many instances this is a practical thing to do, but it does have the disadvantage of absorbing precious time from an already short winter day.

The snowhouse has many advantages over a tent—the most alluring being that it is much warmer. The colder the outside temperature, the greater the advantage. As well, a snowhouse cannot be blown away, and it is soundproof.

The illustrations on the following pages show an ideal method of construction. You can get a great deal of protection against cold and wind simply by excavating a depression in the snow. Sometimes natural bowls under large trees offer ready-made shelter, which needs only a roof. If it becomes necessary to dig a hole in a snow cover and you do not have a shovel, you can use the toe of a snowshoe or any other item that can serve as a scoop. If you can reach bare ground, you will benefit from ground heat. It is also preferable if your excavation is deep enough to allow you to sit up. For the roof, you can use boughs, skis, snowshoes, or your sled. Cover the frame with two large garbage bags (which should be in your personal survival kit), and pile snow on top for insulation. Extra garbage bags or your backpacks can be used to cover the entrance. A few boughs between your body and the ground will prevent body-heat loss due to conduction. It is amazing what can be improvised in an emergency, provided you are not too fatigued or handicapped by physical injury.

Four Basic Snow Shelter Designs

Snow Trench — This is the simplest type of snow shelter and the quickest of all shelters to build, but the ideal dimensions, from a constructional point of view, make it more cramped than other designs. Because the roof span must be kept within a certain maximum dimension a trench does not lend itself well to side-by-side occupancy, but this is possible. The alternative is to consider an end-to-end configuration, with a common entry pit in the middle. This means, of course, that you lose the heat benefit when two bodies are under one roof.

In general, the advantage of the snow trench design is that there is minimal body contact with snow during construction, which means that you stand far less chance of getting wet during the building process. The same goes for the igloo.

To construct a snow trench, you need to find or create deep snow, either by locating a deep drift or by piling snow that is at least 1 metre

ILLUSTRATION 24 — **Single-Person Snow Trench**

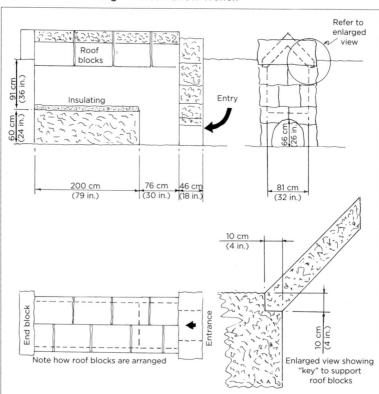

ILLUSTRATION 25 — **Snow Trench**

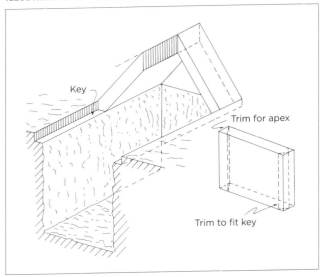

Key

Trim for apex

Trim to fit key

(3 feet) deep. It takes about an hour and a half to build an end-to-end trench for two people and less time for a side-by-side shelter. You should have a shovel, snow saw, or snow knife to construct this type of shelter.

If you need to make a quick emergency shelter and do not have sufficient tools, you can still build a basic shelter by digging a hole in a snowbank deep enough to allow you sit up. Make a roof frame by laying poles, boughs, skis, ski poles, toboggans, or whatever is available to span the excavation. Then cover the framework with a tarp or garbage bags. To finish, pile snow on top to provide insulation. You can cover the entrance with another tarp, and if you have time construct a windbreak of snow to shield the entrance from wind. Do not forget to have insulation under you.

Snowhouse (*Quin-zhee*) — This is the First Nations equivalent of the Inuit igloo and is perhaps the most common type of snow shelter because it can be constructed when there is only 15 centimetres (6 inches) of snow on the ground. It also requires the least expertise, but it has the disadvantage of taking a long time to first mound and then excavate an interior. When snow is tossed through the air to form a mound a natural fusing (**sintering**) of the resettled material takes place after about an hour. We use this time to collect spruce boughs for our bed. If the ambient air temperature is warmer than −15°C (5°F), the mound will have to be tramped to ensure bonding.

It will take two to three hours to construct a *quin-zhee* that will accommodate three people. Body contact with snow is unavoidable and should be allowed for in terms of dress during the excavation process. The method of construction recommended in this manual is one that minimizes snow contact by using an excavation slot. The only tool required is a shovel, but many shelters of this type have been built in emergency situations using snowshoes, tin plates, pieces of plywood, and even mitts wrapped in plastic bags.

ILLUSTRATION 26 — **Snowhouse (*Quin-zhee*)**

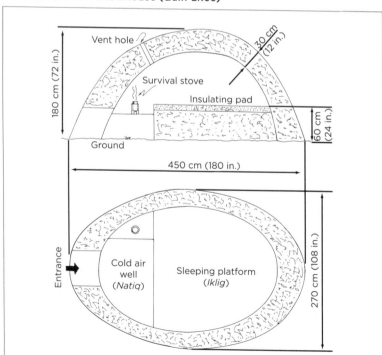

ILLUSTRATION 27 — **How to Build a Snowhouse**

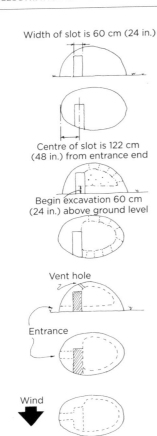

Width of slot is 60 cm (24 in.)

Centre of slot is 122 cm
(48 in.) from entrance end

Begin excavation 60 cm
(24 in.) above ground level

Vent hole

Entrance

Wind

Step 1

a) Mound snow to appropriate
dimensions (refer to drawing) and
allow snow to settle (sinter) for at
least one hour. If there is hoar snow,
trample to hasten settling.

b) Cut excavation slot as shown.

Step 2

a) Place 30 or so sticks, each
30 centimetres (12 inches) long,
all around sleeping area, flush with
outside, as a wall thickness guide
during the excavation process.

b) Excavate from the slot, starting
at a point 60 centimetres (24 inches)
above ground level.

Step 3

a) Fill in excavation slot; using snow
blocks makes this easier.

b) Cut entry hole at ground level, at
right angles to excavation slot. Make
as small as possible.

c) Make vent hole, approximately
5 centimetres (2 inches) in diameter.

Note: Any snow shelter entrance
should be 90 degrees to the wind.

A large quin-zhee.

Snowcave — This is similar in principal to the *quin-zhee* except that you can start excavating without having to mound beforehand. The excavation process for a cave large enough to accommodate three people will take close to two hours. As with construction of a *quin-zhee*, body contact with snow is unavoidable, and you should dress for this during excavation.

ILLUSTRATION 28 — **Snowcave**

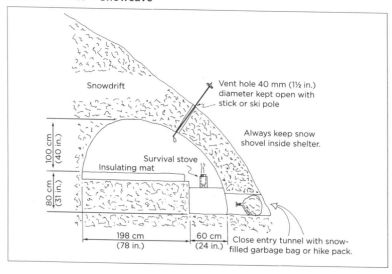

Igloo (*Iglu*) — This is the perfect snowhouse and is not difficult to construct once you know the basics. It also has the advantage of requiring little body contact with the snow during building. The key to construction lies in cutting and placing snow blocks in such a way that they make contact at three points (see illustration below). An igloo that has a 2.4-metre (8-foot) diameter inside dimension will accommodate three people and will take two people the best part of two hours to construct. Of course, as you gain experience, the time frame drops dramatically. Three people building will further reduce the time.

For an igloo you must have a source of hard, wind-packed snow. If you can find snow deposited during a single storm event, this will eliminate all the frustrations introduced by layering or **depth hoar** (a layer of large, very coarse, often hollow crystals).

A little care is required in placing blocks, which should be roughly 66 x 40 x 20 centimetres (26 x 16 x 8 inches). The building process is greatly facilitated if you introduce a single or double spiral, as illustrated.

ILLUSTRATION 29 — **Double-Spiral Igloo**

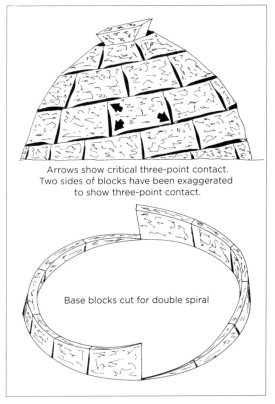

Arrows show critical three-point contact. Two sides of blocks have been exaggerated to show three-point contact.

Base blocks cut for double spiral

*Students taking my winter survival course, held in Yellowknife, NWT,
build a large igloo.*

Common Features of Snow Shelters

Regardless of the type of snow shelter you construct, it must have a sleeping bench (platform) about 0.6 metres (2 feet) higher than the entrance. This will ensure that the sleeping area is the warmest part of the shelter, with the colder (heavier) air lying in the cold well, or entrance pit. Another important feature is a ventilation hole in the roof. This need only be 5 centimetres (2 inches) in diameter and must be watched during occupancy for any closure due to internal icing or external drifting. Keep the entrance to your snow shelter as small as possible so that you can cover it effectively with minimal trouble. A large plastic garbage bag suspended over the entrance and containing a little snow to weigh it down works well. You can have one cover on the outside and another on the inside; a day pack often suffices for the latter. Keep a snow shovel on the inside in case drifted snow blocks the entrance.

I cannot emphasize enough the great benefit afforded by a properly constructed snow shelter. Table 5 says it all. Gaining 30°C or more by using the insulating qualities of snow can mean the difference between life and death.

In a shelter heated by body heat and candles and an entrance that is not airtight, there is no danger of carbon monoxide poisoning as there might be if you were using a gas stove or lantern. The danger of such poisoning is very real because it is undetectable and, therefore, gives you no warning. People have died because they failed to realize the potential danger of gas buildup in such enclosed shelters as snowhouses and tents. While the heat from a gas stove is welcome inside a shelter, there must be a good vent and the stove must burn with an efficient **blue** flame and not a **yellow** one, which indicates incomplete combustion and gives off toxic gas. To avoid the possibility of toxic gas emission, do your gas-stove cooking in the open air.

TABLE 5 — **Snow Shelter Temperatures**

Heat Source	Temperature	
	outside	inside
Good door, single occupant, all night	-19°C (-2°F)	-6°C (21°F)
Good door, two occupants, all night	-49°C (-56°F)	-7°C (19°F)
Good door, two occupants, plus two candles	-44°C (-47°F)	-5°C (23°F)

Note: Temperatures were recorded on the sleeping platform. Shelters had a minimum wall thickness of 20 centimetres (8 inches). The sleeping platform was 60 centimetres (24 inches) above the entrance.

SNOW TOOLS

To build a snow shelter, you need a snow saw or snow knife as well as a shovel. A carpenter's ripsaw with 4.5 to 5 teeth per 2.5 centimetres (1 inch) can be made into a usable snow saw by having the teeth set like a crosscut. Another alternative to a snow saw is a machete. However, I prefer to use one of the following models.

Military Snow Saw — The model used by the military has a high carbon tempered steel blade about 2 millimetres (¹⁄₁₆ inch) in thickness and 41 centimetres (16 inches) in length. The back of the blade is bevelled for part of its length to serve as a snow knife. The 25 mm (one inch) thick laminated wood handle is attached to the blade by means of a twist lock so that it can be carried in two pieces. There are 8 teeth per 12.5 centimetres (5 inches) cut to a depth of 14 millimetres (⁹⁄₁₆ inch). There is no set, and the teeth have bevelled cutting edges similar to those of a crosscut saw. The weight of the saw is quite heavy at 794 grams (28 ounces).

ILLUSTRATION 30 — **Snow Saws**

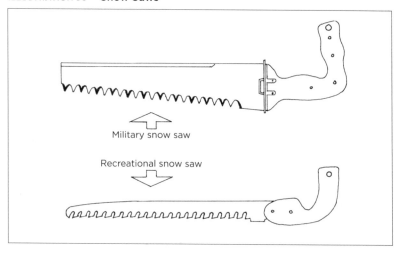

Military snow saw

Recreational snow saw

Lightweight Snow Saw — It is easy to make a very compact, light, and effective snow saw. Using 3-millimetre- (⅛-inch-) thick aluminum, cut out a blade that is 102 millimetres (4 inches) wide and 610 millimetres (24 inches) long. Make the handle from two sections cut out of 13-millimetre (½-inch) plywood, shape accordingly, and, with a spacer in the top half for part of the handle, rivet to the blade. This creates a sturdy handle that is 29 millimetres (1⅛ inches) thick. The entire saw weighs only 454 grams (16 ounces), including the sheath.

ILLUSTRATION 31 — **Snow Saws**

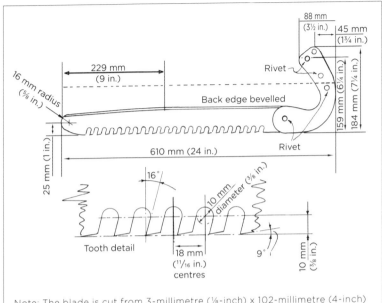

Note: The blade is cut from 3-millimetre (⅛-inch) x 102-millimetre (4-inch) x 610-millimetre (24-inch) aluminum. The handle is in two sections cut out of 13-millimetre (½-inch) plywood with a spacer in the top half.

AVALANCHES

Any discussion of snow would be incomplete without reference to avalanches. All who expect to travel on snow, by whatever means, should have a basic understanding of the metamorphosis of snow when it lies on slopes, especially steep ones. Check for local information about the regional history of avalanches. If you plan to visit mountainous regions for any sport or activity, you would be well advised to enroll in an avalanche course. There is no substitute for hands-on experience and being informed. Motorists driving highways that skirt or pass through mountain ranges should avail themselves of all current weather and road information. Be aware that some mountain ranges, because of their topographic features, are more prone to avalanches than others. Those flanking a maritime weather environment are often the most sensitive and unpredictable.

Avalanche deaths are the most common tragedies that occur in the mountains. The subject of avalanches is very complex. Always err on the side of safety.

Safety Tips for Travel in Avalanche Country

* Always obtain local information. Look for evidence of earlier avalanches, such as a swath through a treed area, a pile of debris, or a carved gulley. Mountaineers usually dig snow pits to observe snow layer stratification in order to obtain a picture of what has gone before and of the stability of the slopes around them.

* Wind plays a big part in creating snow instability on slopes. Windblown material may not bond with the older, underlying, layer.

* Any snow slope greater than 25 degrees can avalanche. Wet snow can move at 15 degrees.

* In many mountainous regions in the world it has always been the practice to cross exposed areas before the sun rises. There are times of the day, and of the year, when avalanches are more likely to occur. South-facing slopes are most dangerous in the spring; north-facing slopes, liable to have depth hoar, are more likely to be active in winter (due to large temperature gradient changes).

* Windward slopes tend to be firmer, with less snow on them. Leeward slopes accumulate snow that is more likely to form slabs, which makes them especially dangerous.

* Slides are more likely to occur within twenty-four hours of a snowfall.

* It is always dangerous to traverse below a cornice.

* Snow-filled gullies, convex slopes, and faces exposed to the afternoon sun, are all dangerous.

* Several people travelling together should cross exposed areas one at a time, with the balance of the party watching from a protected position. A party travelling in line can initiate a slide below its path.

* It is imperative that parties travelling in potential avalanche regions be equipped to carry out a rescue. A buried person can only last a short time before oxygen deprivation takes its toll. Probes, shovels (grain scoops are best), and electronic transceivers should be at hand.

* In addition to basic rescue gear every party member should be familiar with the line-abreast search (probing) method. The speediest rescue from any rescue centre will take too long.

* If you are caught in an avalanche, adopt a swimming motion to keep on top of the snow. When the slide comes to rest, try to thrust an arm in the direction of the surface. Your other hand should, ideally, be in front of the chest and face to create a cavity for breathing.

* Supplement your knowledge of avalanches by reading literature on the subject and by viewing videos. Much reliable information has been published (see Suggested Readings at the end of this book). I strongly recommend the *Avalanche Handbook*, published by the U.S. Department of Agriculture Forest Service. Superb snow and ice traveller and Yukon avalanche consultant Hector Mackenzie speaks well of two videos, *Winning the Avalanche Game* and *Snow Sense*.

chapter 4

TRIP PLANNING AND PREPARATION

THE MOST SUCCESSFUL WILDERNESS exploits are preceded by many hours of detailed planning. While the idea of crossing the Richardson Mountains between Yukon and the Northwest Territories might arise over a bowl of soup at the deli, it is only after you have planned out the logistics of the enterprise—from studying maps to arranging air support to listing gear and packaging food—that the adventure actually begins. There are four basic steps on the organizational ladder:

Step 1

Assess the overall practicality of the trip in terms of:

* terrain
* climate
* time of year
* available equipment
* experience of party members
* physical condition of party members

Define the objectives of the trip in terms of the opportunity to:

* study wildlife

- sketch or photograph a snow-covered landscape
- test certain equipment and travel techniques
- make contact with indigenous people
- enjoy a peaceful and scenic environment in the company of others
- accept a certain physical challenge
- practice using ice and snow for travel and survival

Other recommendations:

- Try to find accounts of journeys over the same route and contact seasoned winter travellers to check feasibility.
- Study topographical maps of a suitable scale (for the hiker, 1:50,000 or 1:250,000 scale). For Canadian topographical maps, write to Canada Map Office, 615 Booth Street, Ottawa, Ontario K1A 0E9. For topographical maps in the United States, write to Branch of Distribution, United States Geological Survey, Federal Center, Denver, Colorado 80225, USA.
- onsider examining aerial photos if maps show insufficient detail (oblique air photos can often help in route finding).

Step 2

Prepare a daily itinerary.

Step 3

Prepare lists of expedition supplies and personal equipment. Here are a few items that a person who is more accustomed to making a trip of similar length in summer might overlook:

- a sturdy, lightweight folding shovel
- a light snow saw (454 grams, or 16 ounces), including sheath
- a Thermos, or insulated bottle
- a headlamp
- a good-quality down sleeping bag rated for sub-zero temperatures and, to lay beneath that, two closed-cell mats (A self-inflating pad like a Therm-a-Rest, is not good enough by itself.)
- an ice probe, to be included in the communal gear should

your route take you across frozen rivers or lakes

* personal clothing and footwear that provides adequate protection against the most extreme weather in the region you are travelling
* fire-lighting materials
* snacks, kept close to the body so that they do not harden in the cold
* surgical tubing (1 metre, or 3 feet), which serves as both a super drinking straw and a handy fire coaxer. Rather than having to place your nose and your parka ruff within a few centimetres of glowing coals, the tube allows a safer technique.

Step 4

Prepare menus, giving particular consideration to the caloric value for the physical demands of the journey and the climate. Make at itemized food list, and package food in daily units for each of the three conventional meals. Allow for on-trail snacks and drinks.

Trip Navigation

Since 1999, when the first edition of this book was published, there have been numerous developments in the field of electronics, notably the GPS (global positioning system) transmitter. This pocket-sized device allows us to transmit a signal that will be reflected back to us by a number of earth-orbiting satellites to give us our geographical coordinates (latitude and longitude). However, it should not replace carrying a map or knowing how to plot a course using a compass and protractor.

One major convenience afforded by a GPS is that it allows us, from the comfort of our home, to identify critical points along our planned route. In the field, we can recall any of those points (waypoints), and the GPS will give us the distance and bearing to that point from our current position. This way, we can traverse from one waypoint to another.

However, we must remember that the GPS gives a straight-line distance between waypoints that goes across canyons, rivers, or other obstacles. This, along with the risk of battery power failure, is reason enough to continue carrying your map, compass, and protractor and know how to use them.

PREPARATION

When preparing for a winter foray, whether it is a day, overnight, weekend, or extended journey, you need to consider the same basic issues:

Team up — Although there are a few advantages to travelling alone, they are far outweighed by the disadvantages, with particular emphasis on safety. It is simply safer to travel in pairs with the optimum party size being four: two can go for help while one remains with the injured.

Winterize your equipment — Ensure that all zippers have ties that are long enough that you can operate them while wearing mittens. If there are any items of gear likely to be left outside, paint them bright orange, red, or blue.

Leave a record — Whether you are a novice or a seasoned pro, you should always leave a detailed itinerary with a responsible person who knows you well. Ideally, this itinerary would include a map with your route clearly marked, and your expected dates of arrival at specific points. It is also recommended that you include a list of the gear you have with you, with details such as the colour of your tent(s) and outer apparel. The more remote and longer the journey, the more detailed the itinerary should be.

THE PERSONAL SURVIVAL KIT

As long as you are appropriately dressed and able to construct a snow shelter, the personal survival kit (PSK) will enable you to survive overnight in the wilderness in winter, without benefit of a sleeping bag, in relative safety. I can say this with confidence because I have done it many times.

The PSK described in this handbook is designed around a unique candle-fired stove, the YuCan. Made from two ordinary, uncoated food cans that nest one inside the other, this stove can be made in two sizes. The smaller unit utilizes a 284-millilitre (10-fluid-ounces) can and a 398-millilitre (14-fluid-ounce) can in combination, whereas the larger model uses a 398-millilitre (14-fluid-ounce) and a 540-millilitre (19-fluid-ounce) can in combination. The more compact unit will accommodate two tea light candles burning side by side, and the larger will accommodate three tea light candles. Which size you choose will depend largely on the way you are travelling. With an eye to minimum weight and bulk, the foot traveller will likely opt for the smaller unit. Those who habitually travel with some form of transport, like a snow-mobile, will most likely prefer to carry the larger model.

An explanation of how such the YuCan stove can be constructed is given on pages 82–83. The unit can be made with simple tools in about an hour. The support for the inside of the can is a rod, or a 20-penny (10-centimetre or 4-inch) nail. If you use a rod, one end should be bent slightly to prevent it from sliding out of the hole in the outer can. If you use a nail, its head does the same thing. While in use, the stove is normally suspended by a small chain attached to the top rim of the larger can (see diagram on page 84).

The design of the stove makes efficient use of the heat from the candles to melt snow or ice for a warm drink, which will help you stay hydrated. The stove also provides heat and light to your shelter. If you use the two-candle version, it will take about 47 minutes to melt snow and obtain hot (not boiling) water. The three-candle version is a little more efficient, reducing the time to 38 minutes. Using the larger can also provides more to drink. Tea light candles can be purchased at many stores, but they vary in quality. Do not buy scented ones. IKEA sells them in bags of one hundred.

When carried in a shoulder pouch, or fanny bag, the stove serves as a container to accommodate nine or twelve long-burning tea lights. The weight of a small YuCan stove and the items recommended to complete the kit will be close to 680 grams (24 ounces). However, the type, size, and weight of the individual components will vary.

Water, Water Everywhere and Not a Drop to Drink

Referring to the diagram on page 84, you will not need much time or tinsmithing experience to construct the YuCan stove. The two sizes illustrated were dictated by the availability of commercial can sizes and the need to satisfy a balance between capacity and compactness. To facilitate the making of such a vital item, the secret is to use an insert (ideally a log) compatible in size with the inside diameter of the can to be worked on. This gives rigidity to the can as you drill, hacksaw, and chisel where necessary.

Because it is difficult to see in the diagram, I should mention that two cutouts (candle entry slots) are made diametrically opposite one another. For the larger can, these slots are the same size, but for the smaller can the candle entry slot is 41 millimetres (1⅝ inch) wide at the entry side and 35 millimetres (1⅜ inch) wide at the other side. This difference allows the tea light to protrude slightly, giving more space for the two candles to nest. Coincident with this shorter dimension is the absence of a lip.

Candle Unit — Eight holes, 6 millimetres (0.25 inch) in size, are drilled where the candle access cutouts are to be made. Using a mini-hacksaw with fine teeth, make horizontal cuts between holes. Using a sharp chisel, make a vertical cut midway between the cuts and press the two sections inwards to lie inside the can against its shell. At this point, two 6-millimetre (0.25-inch) holes are drilled at a specific height diametrically opposite one another to accommodate a support nail or rod that is slightly bent at its point to prevent it from sliding out. To finish, drill two 3-millimitre (0.125-inch) holes at the top of the candle unit, again opposite one another, to permit the attachment of small split rings to which a small link chain can be attached so you can suspend the stove clear of a snow surface or irregular ground.

Container Unit — Use the insert can to collect and melt snow or ice and to drink out of. It is important that the cans used for this purpose are not the internally coated type. Drill 3-millimetre (⅛-inch) holes at the rim of the can to facilitate the attachment of a short length of picture wire. This wire should lie close to the outside of the can so that it will not prohibit the entry of the container into the candle unit. Such a wire will permit suspension over an open fire, if such a heat source is available.

Lid — To conserve heat, make the lid out of a single piece of metal to create a flange that will slide down between the container and the candle unit. This flange will keep the lid from sliding off. When carrying the folded unit, use a piece of duct tape to keep the cap in place.

Contents of the Personal Survival Kit

1. YuCan candle-fired survival stove that doubles as a container when carried
2. long-burning candles (tea lights or tub candles)
3. fire-starter equipment (matches, fire-starter tablets, fire paste, wax plugs, flint, and steel with cotton wool or extra-fine steel wool)
4. four large (leaf-size) garbage bags (preferably blue for visibility)
5. signal mirror (preferably with built-in aiming device)
6. flare gun (pencil type) with red and white flares
7. plastic whistle
8. soup cubes, sugar cubes, and ginger tea
9. braided nylon cord (3 millimetres x 10 metres, or 0.125 inches x 30 feet)

ILLUSTRATION 32 — **YuCan Survival Stove**

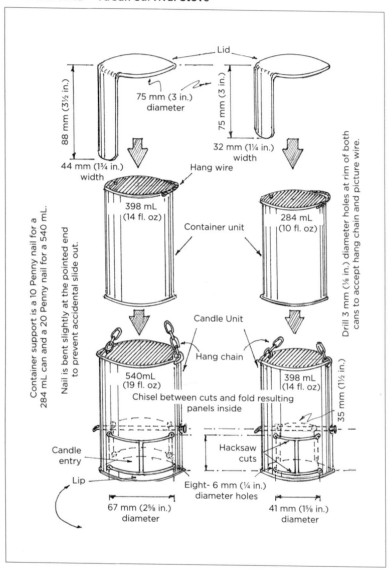

10. snare wire
11. swizzle stick (6 millimetres x 18 centimetres, or 0.25 inches x 7 inches) to stir snow or ice in the drink can so that it will remain in contact with the bottom of the can
12. personal medical supplies (if needed)
13. sunglasses or eye shield
14. waxed dental floss and needle
15. nylon gill net (1 x 6 metres, with 6-centimetre mesh, or 3 x 18 feet, 2⅜-inch mesh)

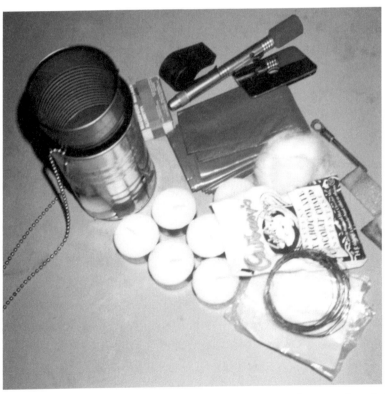

Some contents of a personal survival kit.

Items to Carry on Your Person

1. ground-to-air emergency code (see page 137)
2. pocket knife
3. matches in waterproof container or waterproof matches*
4. toilet tissue (3 metres, or 9 feet)
5. piece of folded waxed paper folded (31 x 31 centimetres, or 1 x 1 foot) to use as fire starter (see page 142)

*Note: Most matches today are poorly made, with flimsy striker pads. Make it a habit to carry waterproof matches in three locations: in the PSK, in a trouser pocket, and in your vehicle or on your sled.

The Day Pack

Most people embarking on a day-long cross-country ski jaunt or snow-mobile trip carry a day pack. Such an item usually contains lunch, a Thermos of tea or cocoa, and a few odds and ends of clothing to accommodate a possible change in weather or an overnight bivouac.

Consider your day pack supplementary to your PSK. With this in mind, you should include a few tools that could be used for shelter construction. To this end, I have made a list of items that, in conjunction with the PSK, will see you through the worst scenario.

While this list might seem overly burdensome at first glance, if you take care to select lightweight gear the day pack should weigh little more than 5 kilograms (11 pounds).

Some of the equipment can be shared among your companions so that the whole concept of carrying emergency gear becomes more acceptable. If you are an off-road traveller in a land of snow and cold temperatures, you must carry some means of excavating or mounding snow to build a shelter. This may range from a piece of plywood to the latest in high-tech folding shovels. I strongly recommend that anyone contemplating winter travel in remote areas, regardless of their mode of transportation, have with them the best possible lightweight, compact folding shovel that money can buy. No cheapies,

ILLUSTRATION 33 — **Two Important Items: Folding Shovel and Tea Light**

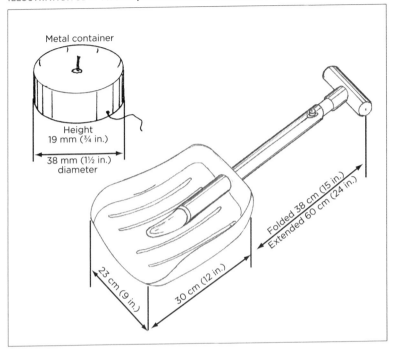

Metal container

Height
19 mm (¾ in.)

38 mm (1½ in.)
diameter

Folded 38 cm (15 in.)
Extended 60 cm (24 in.)

23 cm (9 in.)

30 cm (12 in.)

please! You want an implement that will be strong, well made of light materials, and portable.

Contents of Day Pack:

1. lightweight shovel (good quality, folding)
2. lightweight over pants (breathable yet waterproof)
3. lightweight silk, fleece, or wool scarf
4. lightweight down booties
5. lightweight down jacket
6. foam pad (preferably made of Evazote)
7. bivouac sack
8. mini-first-aid kit
9. wool or fleece socks (can serve as mitts in an emergency)
10. additional tea light candles
11. mini-flashlight or headlamp

12. emergency food (e.g. Logan bread, fruit cake or shortbread)
13. light, tight-weave cloth, at least 3 metres (10 feet) square
14. snow saw or snow knife
15. candle lantern
16. insulated flask for water or Thermos
17. garbage bags with holes for arms and head, to be used as a wetsuit when excavating a snow shelter. Also useful as a vapour-barrier garment, a snow shelter door, or laid on top of a roof support frame of a snow trench prior to covering with snow
18. rubber drinking tube (6 millimetres x 30 centimetres, or 0.2 x 12 inches diameter)
19. stub pencil and single sheet of paper from writing pad
20. neck gaiter that can be pulled up to serve as face mask
21. pee bottle (because there is nothing worse than disturbing your companion and breaking the insulation of your shelter entrance simply to empty your bladder)

chapter 5

~

LIVING WITH COLD

FEW OF US WHO are exposed to a cold environment for at least half the year give much thought to the fact that we are not physiologically designed to live there. We are homeotherms, handicapped by the need to maintain a **body core temperature** of 37°C (98.6°F). In other words we must rely on clothing and a protective shelter to survive in all but a subtropical environment. On the plus side, our body is equipped with its own protective mechanisms, some that we feel and many that we do not, which attempt to maintain core temperature at its optimum. It is our responsibility to understand these involuntary systems so that we can help and not hinder their chance of success.

THE BODY'S PROTECTIVE MECHANISMS

Of the defence mechanisms that can be felt when the body is exposed to cold, we are certainly aware of at least two: goose bumps (**pilo erection**) and shivering. The former is not too effective, but the latter is highly so. We are not cognizant of processes initiated by signals sent to the brain from censors located in various parts of the body. Foremost among these processes is the body's ability to regulate the flow of blood through the circulatory system in such a manner that such vital organs as the brain, heart, lungs, liver, and kidneys are ensured an adequate supply of warm blood. When cold temperatures pose a threat to core temperature, **vasomotor action** constricts appropriate arteries so that circulating blood is shunted to preserve the status quo. This means that flow to the extremities will be short circuited to protect the core. This is one of the reasons why hands and feet so readily succumb to frostbite. In concert with the thermoregulation of blood, and at the command of the autonomic nervous system, hormones will be released to stimulate pulse, metabolic activity and muscle tone. The combined effect of these defence mechanisms helps a great deal in protecting us from hypothermia.

Yet we must take whatever action possible to prevent the loss of body heat and to preserve core temperature. A drop of just 2°C (36°F) in core temperature will already impair body functions, and Table 6 shows quite dramatically what little room we have to spare. It is no exaggeration to say that survival comes down to keeping warm and remaining hydrated.

While the acquisition of food is not a priority in a short-term emergency situation, it is imperative that we remain hydrated at all times. As soon as we become dehydrated, many of the body's functions are impaired, including those that fight against hypothermia. This is, of course, easier said than done when snow and ice are all around us. That is why it is imperative that any PSK contains matches and a candle stove that will, in the absence of fire, facilitate the melting of snow or ice and provide a warm drink.

While our body can be warmed from such external sources as the sun (short-wave radiation) and fire (long-wave radiation), we obtain internal heat from the body's defence mechanism of shivering, from exercise, and from the metabolic conversion of food. Unfortunately, we can lose heat in ways that are far more insidious.

The greatest loss occurs through **radiation**, whereby electromagnetic energy (including heat) is able to travel through space at the speed of light (infrared transmission).

Everything radiates heat. Because of the principle that heat moves along a gradient, the waves from the warmer object dominate. The amount of heat loss depends on the surface area exposed and the difference between skin and air temperature. The loss may be lessened when parts of the body radiate to each other: finger to finger (that is why mitts are more effective than gloves in keeping your hands warm) or leg to leg. When you are in a fetal position, some surface areas will radiate heat one to the other. At the other end of the scale, the neck, face, and some say the head are the most efficient **heat sinks** and should be given priority protection.

We can lose heat by **conduction** through the interaction of molecules and atoms. This requires actual physical contact. Conduction occurs within our bodies. Heat is conducted from our exercising muscles to the skin surface. To conserve this heat, it is important to avoid contact with cold objects and guard against wet clothing. The greatest potential danger is being partially or totally immersed in cold water. The rate of heat loss in this instance is likely to be twenty-five times greater than that which occurs one is standing in air of the same temperature. We tend to forget that heat is lost to the ground through the soles of boots. The selection of effective footwear, with good sole insulation, is of the utmost importance.

Evaporation is a process that plays a significant part in the fight to conserve body heat during cold weather. Any sweat that may be created by physical activity will be vaporized by body heat. The problem is that the vaporizing of perspiration uses up valuable calories, which could lower body temperature below a safe level.

We can also lose heat through **respiration**. Inhaling cold, dry air and exhaling warm, moist air does little to preserve a vital core temperature. The deep hood of a parka or some form of protecting shield

ILLUSTRATION 34 — **Critical Areas for Heat Loss**

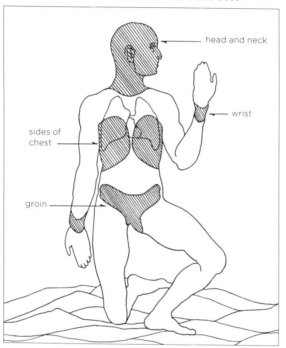

across the face is helpful. In order to keep losses through evaporation and respiration within safe bounds, it is important to move in such a manner that sweating and deep, fast, breathing are kept to a minimum.

Yet another way we can lose heat is through **convection**, which is a special type of conduction. The term refers to situations in which one of two substances is in motion. This circulation process is aided by the propensity of heat to rise. Rough surfaces cause turbulence, which slows the movement of air (remember the body's defence mechanism of goosebumps). While heat transfer is always from a warmer to a colder object, the loss is accentuated by convection.

To further clarify Illustration 35, the hypothalamus receives signals from sensors located in various parts of the body. It then relays such signals to the cerebral cortex, which has the function of integrating complex sensory and neural functions before passing such

ILLUSTRATION 35 — **The Body's Sensors and Defence Mechanisms: How the Body Maintains Core Temperatures**

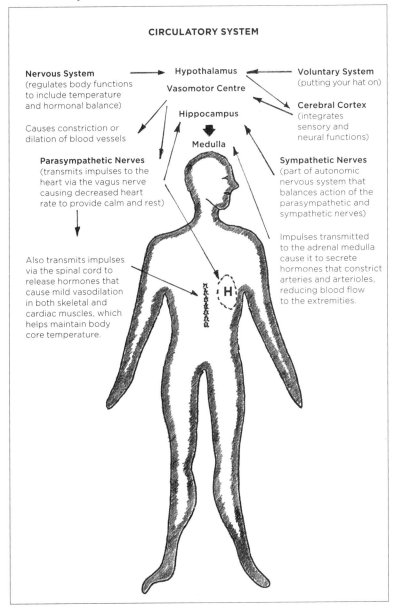

CIRCULATORY SYSTEM

Nervous System (regulates body functions to include temperature and hormonal balance)

Causes constriction or dilation of blood vessels

Parasympathetic Nerves (transmits impulses to the heart via the vagus nerve causing decreased heart rate to provide calm and rest)

Also transmits impulses via the spinal cord to release hormones that cause mild vasodilation in both skeletal and cardiac muscles, which helps maintain body core temperature.

Hypothalamus

Vasomotor Centre

Hippocampus

Medulla

Voluntary System (putting your hat on)

Cerebral Cortex (integrates sensory and neural functions)

Sympathetic Nerves (part of autonomic nervous system that balances action of the parasympathetic and sympathetic nerves)

Impulses transmitted to the adrenal medulla cause it to secrete hormones that constrict arteries and arterioles, reducing blood flow to the extremities.

H

information to the vasomotor centre. The latter transmits impulses, via parasympathetic nerves, to the heart by way of the vagus nerve. Such impulses cause a decreased heart rate to provide calm and rest. At the same time, the hippocampus, as the centre of our protective autonomic nervous system, will balance the action of these parasympathetic impulses with those emanating from the sympathetic system before they are transmitted to the adrenal medulla. This enables the medulla to secrete hormones that constrict arteries and arterioles, thus reducing blood flow to the extremities. To afford appropriate regulation and protection, the parasympathetic nerves transmit impulses, via the spinal cord, to release hormones that cause vasodilation in both skeletal and cardiac muscles. The combined effect of such control mechanisms will help the body maintain its proper body core temperature unless by neglect, or unavoidable accident, we stress our autonomic protection system beyond its limit. As the body's immune system protects against disease, so it is, via such defence mechanisms, that the body can maintain its critical core temperature.

WINDCHILL

The **windchill index** is a measure of the combined effect of air speed and temperature as it affects the human body. The degree of heat deprivation depends on the surface area of the exposed skin and on the windchill factor. This effect is logarithmic with two-thirds of the cooling effect of windchill occurring in the first 3 kilometres per hour. The entire windchill factor is greatly magnified (thirty-four times) in the presence of high humidity. The primary function of clothing is to reduce convection and trap a layer of warm, still air next to the skin.

It is usually the atmospheric environment that dictates where we go, how we get there, and what we do when we arrive. Since we humans may be classified as both endotherms (warm-blooded) and homeotherms (in need of a constant inner core temperature), how we function in a predominantly cold, hostile region depends on what clothing gives us the best protection and what items we take, in the way of protective and emergency equipment that will also ensure safe passage. The effect of wind, especially in sub-zero temperatures, has an overwhelming influence on one's comfort and safety.

Several formulas have been developed to provide an index of windchill, but because there are so many factors to consider (many of them relating to the condition of the individual) any guide must be used with caution. However, some quantification is better than none at all, and it is in this light that the tables and nomogram, based on a recently developed formula, have been included with this text.

Wind speed and actual thermometer readings are converted into an equivalent thermometer reading. For example, −5°C (23°F) with a wind speed of 40 kilometres per hour is equivalent to being exposed to −14°C (7°F) with no wind. Table 6 relates such temperature-like values to frostbite exposure times.

When the first edition of this book came out in 1999, I included a table, a nomogram, and a way to classify windchill based on a relationship between windchill and its effect on exposed skin. In 2001, in the wake of an international workshop with more than four hundred participants from thirty-five countries, a new methodology for determining windchill was developed. A team of scientists and medical experts from Canada and the United States worked together to develop a new index, based on the loss of heat from the face, the part of the body most exposed to severe winter weather. The formula developed in 2001 estimates wind speed based on observations of the movement of such objects as trees and flats. It is considered more accurate than any that had been used before.

TABLE 6 — **Little Room to Spare**

Body Core Temperature	Reaction
37°C (98.6°F)	normal body core temperature
36°C (97°F)	shivering—time to take action
35°C (95°F)	hard shivering—coordination decreases
33°C (91°F)	violent shivering—loss of ability to move muscles; loss of ability to reason
31°C (88°F)	unconsciousness
24°C (75°F)	death (in most cases)

TABLE 7 — **Windchill: How Strong Is It? Look around You!**

To Help us Estimate Wind Speed	Wind Speed	
	km/h	mph
smoke and wind vanes indicate wind directions; wind felt on face	10	6
small flags are extended; small twigs in motion	20	12
large flags flap; branches of small trees move; loose snow rises	30	18
large flags are fully extended; small trees in leaf sway	40	24
branches of large trees move; whistling heard in overhead wires	50	31
tops of large trees bend; wind is an impediment to walking	60	37
considerable drifting of snow; twigs break off trees	65	40
loose objects could become airborne	70	43
tree branches break off; slight damage to structures	75	46
at 88 to 101 km/h trees are uprooted; much damage to structures	80	49

TABLE 8 — Windchill Chart for Canadian Residents

T air = air temperature in °C and V_{10} = observed wind speed at 10m elevation, in km/h.

T air / V_{10} (km/h)	5°	0°	-5°	-10°	-15°	-20°	-25°	-30°	-35°	-40°	-45°	-50°
5	4	-2	-7	-13	-19	-24	-30	-36	-41	-47	-53	-58
10	3	-3	-9	-15	-21	-27	-33	-39	-45	-51	-57	-63
15	2	-4	-11	-17	-23	-29	-35	-41	-48	-54	-60	-66
20	1	-5	-12	-18	-24	-30	-37	-43	-49	-56	-62	-68
25	1	-6	-12	-19	-25	-32	-38	-44	-51	-57	-64	-70
30	0	-6	-13	-20	-26	-33	-39	-46	-52	-59	-65	-72
35	0	-7	-14	-20	-27	-33	-40	-47	-53	-60	-66	-73
40	-1	-7	-14	-21	-27	-34	-41	-48	-54	-61	-68	-74
45	-1	-8	-15	-21	-28	-35	-42	-48	-55	-62	-69	-75
50	-1	-8	-15	-22	-29	-35	-42	-49	-56	-63	-70	-76
55	-2	-8	-15	-22	-29	-36	-43	-50	-57	-63	-71	-78
60	-2	-9	-16	-23	-30	-36	-43	-50	-58	-65	-72	-79
65	-2	-9	-16	-23	-30	-37	-44	-51	-58	-65	-72	-80
70	-2	-9	-16	-23	-30	-37	-44	-51	-58	-65	-72	-80
75	-3	-10	-17	-24	-31	-38	-45	-52	-59	-66	-73	-80
80	-3	-10	-17	-24	-31	-38	-45	-52	-60	-67	-74	-81

The Old Farmer's Almanac, almanac.com

FROSTBITE GUIDE

Low risk of frostbite for most people

Increasing risk of frostbite for most people in 10 to 30 minutes of exposure

High risk for most people in 5 to 10 minutes of exposure

High risk for most people in 2 to 5 minutes of exposure

High risk for most people in 2 minutes of exposure or less

TABLE 9 – Windchill Chart for United States Residents

TEMPERATURE (°F)

CALM	40	35	30	25	20	15	10	5	0	-5	-10	-15	-20	-25	-30	-35	-40	-45
5	36	31	25	19	13	7	1	-5	-11	-16	-22	-28	-34	-40	-46	-52	-57	-63
10	34	27	21	15	9	3	-4	-10	-16	-22	-28	-35	-41	-47	-53	-59	-66	-72
15	32	25	19	13	6	0	-7	-13	-19	-26	-32	-39	-45	-51	-58	-64	-71	-77
20	30	24	17	11	4	-2	-9	-15	-22	-29	-35	-42	-48	-55	-61	-68	-74	-81
25	29	23	16	9	3	-4	-11	-17	-24	-31	-37	-44	-51	-58	-64	-71	-78	-84
30	28	22	15	8	1	-5	-12	-19	-26	-33	-39	-46	-53	-60	-67	-73	-80	-87
35	28	21	14	7	0	-7	-14	-21	-27	-34	-41	-48	-55	-62	-69	-76	-82	-89
40	27	20	13	6	-1	-8	-15	-22	-29	-36	-43	-50	-57	-64	-71	-78	-84	-91
45	26	19	12	5	-2	-9	-16	-23	-30	-37	-44	-51	-58	-65	-72	-79	-86	-93
50	26	19	12	4	-3	-10	-17	-24	-31	-38	-45	-52	-60	-67	-74	-81	-88	-95
55	25	18	11	4	-3	-11	-18	-25	-32	-39	-46	-54	-61	-68	-75	-82	-89	-97
60	25	17	10	3	-4	-11	-19	-26	-33	-40	-48	-55	-62	-69	-76	-84	-91	-98

WIND (MPH)

FROSTBITE TIMES: 30 minutes   10 minutes   5 minutes

Wind Chill (°F) = 35.74 + 0.6215T - 35.75(V$^{0.16}$) + 0.4275T(V$^{0.16}$) where T = Air Temperature (°F) V = Wind Speed (mph)

TABLE 10 — **Windchill (Brr! Brr!)**

General Qualification	Wind Chill Temperatures		Safety Advisory
	°C	°F	
low danger	0 to -10	0 to 14	Dress warmly in winter clothing (not cotton or jeans), wear hat, scarf and insulated gloves.
moderate danger	-11 to -25	12 to -13	Wear hat, neck cover, mitts, winter boots; layers of insulated clothing with wool must have a breathable but windproof outer shell. Risk of hypothermia with prolonged exposure.
need for care	-26 to -45	-15 to -49	Keep active, cover all skin since frostbite possible if exposed, need to check often. Skin can freeeze at temperatures between -40°C and -47°C in 5 to 10 min. Take frequent warm-up periods. Risk of hypothermia if prolonged exposure and especially if wet.
extreme	-46 to -59	-51 to -76	Highly uncomfortable, outdoor activity should be limited to short periods, cover all exposed skin which can freeze in 2 min. Serious risk of hypothermia.
very extreme	-60 and colder		Outdoor exposure is extremely hazardous. Best advice is to remain in a warm shelter.

HYPOTHERMIA

Just a few decades ago, few of us would have been familiar with the word hypothermia. When people succumbed to cold it was usually reported that they had died of exposure. We are discussing a circumstance where the body core temperature has fallen below its normal operating level of 37°C (98.6°F). Body core refers to the body's vital organs such as the brain, heart, lungs, kidneys, and liver.

The vascular system acts as a radiator in the human body. When the hypothalamus (the temperature-sensing organ in the brain) receives a message that the body is too warm, blood circulation to the skin and the extremities is increased so that excess heat can be lost. If, on the other hand, the message is that the body is cold, then blood vessels to the extremities constrict, short-circuiting the normal pattern of flow, so that warm blood will continue to circulate within the core region. It is through this vasoconstriction and vasodilation of blood vessels to the extremities that the heart will be protected against the passage of cold blood that it cannot tolerate.

Although the body will induce goosebumps and shivering to protect itself and warn us that we are approaching a hypothermic state, it is a fact that we are less likely to recognize signs that are more readily observed by our travel companion.

Our travel companion will notice a slurring of our speech or will observe that we have stumbled twice in the last 100 metres (328 feet) and that we have fumbled with our ski harness instead of adjusting it quickly. Should you need to make travel decisions, your companion will recognize that you are not reasoning very well. The situation is the same in the case of frostbite. Someone else will tell you that the tip of your nose is white and frozen, something that you will not be aware of. This is one of several reasons why it is crucial to travel in pairs.

Treatment

Treating a person with hypothermia in the field is not easy. In fact, only mild hypothermia, recognized by shivering among other signs, is treatable in a wilderness setting. Shivering is not only an effective recovery mechanism, creating internal warmth, but is also a useful indicator of the stage of hypothermia that an individual may have reached. If shivering stops while the person is showing increased alertness, the core temperature must be rising; if shivering ceases coincident with a decrease in consciousness, then their core temperature is falling. If the person is unresponsive (without obvious head trauma but with detectable pulse and respiration) and not shivering, core temperature is likely to be below 32°C (90°F), which would signify profound hypothermia.

At this point, we have to re-warm the victim as speedily as possible, and the way we accomplish this will depend on our knowledge and what resources are available.

First, dry clothing sufficiently to afford adequate insulation, and replace any that is wet.

Second, have the victim lie down, horizontally with feet slightly elevated, in a way that he or she is effectively insulated from cold air and ground. Sleeping bags, blankets, and perhaps a vapour barrier should be used to ensure no further heat loss can occur through radiation, conduction, and convection. It is important to cover the head, neck, and face. Third, if the person is responsive, you can administer a warm sweetened drink, but not one that contains caffeine, which is a diuretic, or alcohol. Do not permit smoking because this will result in vasoconstriction at a time when we need an adequate blood flow.

Other methods of warming up a person at risk of hypothermia is to transfer heat from a warm person to a cold one by sharing a sleeping bag, administering hot water bottles, or allowing the patient to inhale steam from heated water. Once the victim has been showing signs of improvement for about an hour, he or she could benefit from some exercise to warm up the body.

Note that the foregoing relies heavily on the autonomic shivering process to re-warm the victim. Be careful not to warm the skin to the extent that receptors there will send "all-is-well" signals to the thermoregulatory centre. That will result in a premature suppression of the shivering mechanism.

A person with more profound hypothermia must be given more specialized recovery treatment. Certainly give them the treatment outlined above, but also make every possible move to secure professional help, medical assistance, and more specialized equipment. Never leave a hypothermia victim unattended. As well, do not administer sedatives, tranquilizers, painkillers, aspirin, or other medications; do not massage, rub, or jostle the victim. If you do transport a patient to a facility, be sure that the person is fully protected from cold air and wind (including wind from helicopter blades).

Afterdrop is the term given to continued decline in core temperature despite the fact that a warming of the victim is in progress. The problem is that there is a chance that cold acidic blood from the extremities can be allowed to circulate prematurely before a sufficient warming of the whole body. Re-warming must be systematic and gradual, beginning with the trunk, where vital organs are located. If blood circulation is accelerated by exercise, forcing as-yet-unwarmed blood from the cold extremities to reach the heart, the result can be fatal.

There is an account of sailors being rescued from a life raft after their vessel was torpedoed during the Battle of the Atlantic in the Second World War. The rescue vessel had lowered boarding nets, which the survivors were compelled to climb. It was this exercise that forced cold blood to circulate prematurely, which the heart could not tolerate. The men died of heart failure upon reaching the deck.

The part of the body to be given priority in the re-warming process must always be the trunk and the head. When that region is warm, blood from the extremities can be accepted in the vascular system without causing a strain on the heart and other vital organs.

The processes that may be used at a medical facility include hot tub immersion (with very controlled water temperature regulation); the application of chemical and electrical heat packs; heat cradles; microwave warming; neck coils; warm water beds and other processes that demand special equipment, professional administration, and monitoring.

Anyone treating a victim of hypothermia should be aware that signs of life are not always discernable; the pulse may be so low that is cannot be readily detected. There is a saying that a person cannot be presumed dead unless warm and dead.

FROSTBITE

Treat superficial frostbite by placing a warm hand gently against the affected part; do not rub with your hand or with snow. Cold feet might have to be placed in contact with a warm part of another person. Placing cold feet on your companion's warm tummy can not only be effective physiologically but also serve as a true test of friendship.

For deeply frostbitten limbs, the best solution is to let them remain frozen until medical services can be reached. *On no account should a thawing and re-freezing process be allowed to take place.* For the most part, the body will do what it can to save the affected part and it should be given time to do that under the professional eye of medical authorities.

When it comes to hypothermia and frostbite, prevention is the key. Better to carry a few extra items of clothing for emergencies, pocket your ego and turn back when the weather sours, and seek the closest refuge. Always keep an eye on your companions and take immediate action at the first signs of hypothermia. Remember that frostbite and hypothermia go hand in hand.

A pilot makes soup while the team carries out hydrometric surveys on the Kaskawulsh River.

chapter 6

~

KEEPING WARM

CLOTHING

TO SURVIVE IN A cold environment we endotherms, lacking fur or other natural insulation, must cover our body with insulating garments that will prevent body-heat loss and serve as an effective barrier against the wind. Using caribou, polar bear and seal skins for their protection, the Inuit have demonstrated that it is possible for human beings to live and thrive in the most hostile environment in the world.

With no caribou or polar bears in our backyard those of us who reside in regions subject to long cold winters are at the mercy of the textile industry. A good segment of the population has the sense to procure adequate clothing, while others, succumbing to the whims of the fashion world, expose themselves unnecessarily to discomfort by wearing apparel made of material that does not protect against the cold.

Among circumpolar peoples, Canadians in general rank low in their ability to choose clothing suitable for winter. Russians and Scandinavians accept their nordicity and dress in a way that shows they understand the body's vulnerability to cold. You don't see too many Russians without a fur hat in wintertime, while Canadians have a tendency to go bareheaded.

North Americans generally rely too heavily on support systems such as centrally heated houses and heated automobiles. Some people avoid winter's bite by exposing themselves as little as possible to the outside environment. Flitting from one warm cocoon to another, they hardly change their dress habits as they pass from season to season; jeans and running shoes are worn all year round—which is fine as long as the electricity doesn't go off or the engine doesn't fail.

The danger lies in becoming too complacent. Many people, especially those who are naïve about the dangers of frostbite and hypothermia, would be in an extremely vulnerable position if they had to make an unexpected journey through a relatively isolated region in winter.

In order to dress for cold in the most efficient way, it is imperative to understand a few fundamentals. By having some knowledge of the way our body functions, and the many ways that heat can be drained from it, we are better able to give priority to those areas most sensitive to cold. For instance we know that a great deal of body heat can be lost through an exposed face, neck, and head. In addition to the need for a scarf and hat, there should be some protection for the wrists, groin, and sides of the chest. At the same time we must ensure that neither the weight nor tightness of our apparel will in any way inhibit circulation. We must remember that any **dead air** trapped within (as with a coarse-weave fabric) and between layers of clothing will function as additional insulation. Considering such criteria, it is easy to see remember the three Ls of polar clothing: light, layered, and loose.

In addition to increasing the insulation value of our cover by trapping air between several layers, there is another advantage to multiplicity: it allows us to regulate our dress to compensate for high levels of activity that promote sweating. In a polar environment, it is essential to keep perspiration to a minimum. Not only do we lose body heat as it vaporizes body moisture, but when our garments are wet they lose some of their insulating qualities. To realize maximum efficiency in our clothing, we must do two things: obey the dress code and select the proper materials.

The Dress Code

Three layers are required to adequately protect the body, and each one performs a specific function:

Vapour transmission layer — The layer next to the skin should be of a material that will absorb or **wick** the body moisture (sweat) that forms constantly on the skin. Recommended materials are wool (preferably Merino), silk, polypropylene, Capilene, and Duofold to name a few. Avoid cotton because it takes time to dry, feels terribly cold when wet, and does not wick well.

Insulation layer — The second layer, or layers, insulates us from the cold by trapping body heat. Recommended materials are wool (Shetland or Merino wool is especially light and fast drying), fleece, pile, down, and several synthetic fibres.

Protection layer — The third (outer) layer should be of a material that does not allow wind, or in some instances water, to penetrate. Recommended materials are polyester-cotton blend, uncoated nylon, Gore-Tex, Entrant, Super Microloft. Early-twentieth-century polar explorers used tight-weave Egyptian cotton, like Grenfell cloth, which is also very effective.

The first two layers prevent loss of heat through radiation and the cooling effect produced by the evaporation of body moisture, while the third layer must be windproof, stemming heat loss due to convection, and breathable, allowing body moisture to escape.

Proper Materials

Fortunately, we now have a choice of materials that will perform each one of these functions very well, and I am sure that better materials will follow. Although old-time trappers managed in their wool long johns, heavy wool pants, wool shirts, sweaters, and a tight-weave cotton shell parkas, today we have a wide selection of stronger, lighter, and more effective clothing.

Tips for Cold-Weather Clothing

* Dark-coloured winter clothing absorbs solar radiation, keeping you warmer. A dark garment dries quicker and can be more readily spotted by a search party.

* When cotton worn next to the skin becomes soaked with perspiration, it feels cold and takes a long time to dry. To make matters worse, tight-fitting jeans can restrict circulation. Cotton is not a winter fabric, so leave the jeans, T-shirts, and cotton long johns at home.

* Materials such as polypropylene and wool feel warm when wet and will wick the sweat away from your skin or, in the case of wool, absorb it.

* If ice builds up on your clothing, turn it inside out and beat it with a ski pole.

* Keep batteries, GPS, or phones inside a warm pocket. Seemingly dead batteries may just be cold ones. Select alkaline or superior lithium batteries, which last longer and perform better at low temperatures.

* Cheap mittens are warmer than the most expensive gloves, as fingers conduct heat to one another. Keep your mittens tied to a cord around your neck.

* Wear wristlets, which can be made by cutting off the top 15 centimetres (6 inches) of heavy wool socks.

* When travelling, always move at a pace that minimizes sweating and keep alternating the layers of your clothing.

* A waist sash around a windproof cagoule (light, hooded, windproof garment pulled over the head) in combination with a neck cord will help regulate ventilation.

* All zippers should have pull tabs long enough to make them easy to control with a mitt-covered hand.

* Beware of sunlight reflected from a white surface, even on an overcast day. Have sunscreen and eye protection handy.

* When you feel cold in any part of your body, stop to warm that part.

* Keep your neck and head covered at all times, and carry face mask in your pocket.

* If you are wearing a "warm-dry" type of footwear (see page 118), be sure to dry socks, liners, and insoles overnight. Not only are feet the body parts most sensitive to cold, but they are also the most difficult to protect.

* A headlamp is not a luxury when you consider how few daylight hours there are in winter, especially in northern latitudes.

* In addition to a down sleeping bag with appropriate cold rating, place two closed-cell insulating pads under your sleeping bag to prevent heat loss through conduction. A single self-inflating pad, like a Therm-a-Rest, is not the best choice when you are sleeping on snow.

* Fleece dries faster and is more resistant to wear than wool.

* Although down can provides the best insulation and is highly compressible for packing, it loses its insulation value when it gets wet, and it is very difficult to dry. Many synthetic fills perform much the same way as down and continue to provide insulation when wet.

What Does All This Mean?

In recent decades, the textile industry has been coming up with new materials that manufacturers claim are stronger, lighter, more waterproof, windproof, or breathable than any before. Nowadays, our clothing reflects the brilliance of the chemist more than it does the availability of something that nature has given us. The exceptions are of course wool and down, whose insulation properties cannot be matched. To help you make these choices and better interpret the clothing catalogues, here are definitions of a few terms commonly used in the textile industry:

Acrylic — A soft, colourfast, washable synthetic fibre derived from poly-acrylonitrile. Used in base-layer and insulating fabrics.

BiPolar — A relatively new fabric that uses different weaving techniques, yarn types, and chemical treatments on each side of the fabric. This creates a two-faced fabric that reacts to the different conditions on each side of the surface.

Boiled wool — Wool that has been hot-washed and felted (brushed and compressed) to give it a tighter, more weather-resistant weave. It is less susceptible to extreme shrinking than plain wool weaves.

Capilene — A treated polyester base-layer fabric. The fibre surface is treated to make it hydrophilic, while the core remains hydrophobic. The combination lifts water away from the skin toward outer clothing layers without soaking the fibre.

Continuous filament — A term that describes a yarn made up of indefinitely continuous fibres. Used mostly in synthetic insulations.

Cordura — An abrasion-resistant, air-texturized nylon fabric usually used for making backpacks.

Denier — A measurement of fibre weight used to express the yield and/or thickness of a thread or yarn. Higher denier means larger fibres and stronger material.

Down — The soft undercoating feathers of geese and ducks. Naturally warm, soft and lightweight when dry, but useless when wet. Used in insulating garments and sleeping bags.

Dryloft — A two-ply laminated shell fabric designed specifically for insulating parkas and sleeping bags. It is totally windproof and roughly twice as breathable as Gore-Tex, but only a third as waterproof.

E.C.O. Fleece — A synthetic fleece made from 89 percent recycled soda bottles.

Eco-Pile — A synthetic fleece that is 100 percent post-consumer recycled material from plastic soda bottles.

Ecospun — A fibre made from 80 percent recycled plastic bottles and 20 percent virgin polyester.

Entrant — An elastic, waterproof polyurethane coating that breathes through microscopic pores left during application. Entrant's trade-off between waterproofing and breathability depends on coating thickness—more coating equals more waterproofing and less breathability.

Fleece — Commonly used generic name for pile synthetic fabrics like Polartec.

Gore-Tex — Gore's microporous membrane, when laminated to an outer fabric, keeps rain out while allowing perspiration vapour to escape. Garments of three-layer construction look like a single layer of fabric, but are really a sandwich of Gore-Tex membrane laminated to one of a variety of tough outer fabrics and backed by a protective tricot inner face. Two-layer construction mates the Gore-Tex membrane and an outer fabric with a free-hanging liner.

H₂No — A waterproof/breathable coating that comes in two versions: "Plus" is more breathable but less waterproof; "Storm" is less breathable but more waterproof.

Hollofil — A single-hole polyester insulation for sleeping bags and apparel, most often found in bargain brands. Hollofil II is a four-hole version that is slightly warmer than an equal amount of regular Hollofil, with improved stuffability.

Hydrophilic — A term meaning "water loving" that is often used to describe the wicking characteristics of fabrics.

Hydrophobic — A term meaning "water hating" that is used to describe the water-repellent characteristics of shell fabric and the moisture management or push–pull qualities of underwear fabric.

Lifa Prolite — A polypropylene underlayer fabric distinguished by a soft brushed finish that is not as scratchy as some other polypro garments and is more odour-resistant than most.

Lite Loft — A high-loft, lightweight, 77.5 percent polyester/22.5 percent olefin insulation used in sleeping bags and outerwear.

Loft — The natural ability of wool, down, or other material to hold air, which allows it to act as insulation.

Merino wool — An ultra-soft, non-itchy, strong, durable, lightweight, naturally fire-resistant wool.

Microloft — A polyester insulation made of microfine fibres thinner than a human hair. The dense structure is supposed to trap heat more efficiently than other synfills of equal thickness, and it is supposed to be highly water resistant.

Nylon — The generic term for fibre made from synthetic polyamides extracted from coal and oil. Coated nylon is covered with urethane on the inside to make it waterproof. Nylon cannot be relied on for full water protection without sealed seams, but it is light, packable, durable, and generally low priced.

Olefin — Also known as polypropylene, a propylene/ethylene-based synthetic fibre that is hydrophobic, quick drying, colourfast, and has good heat retention. Subject to shrinkage and sudden meltdown in hot dryers.

Oxford Nylon — A super heavy-duty nylon, usually 200 denier.

Push-pull fabric — A two-part fabric made of nonabsorbent hydrophobic knit next to the skin and absorbent hydrophilic knit on the outside; most often it is polyester on the inside, nylon on the outside.

Packcloth — A nylon fabric of medium weave with a urethane coating on the back to give it water repellency.

Pile — A generic name for synthetic fleece, often used to describe single-sided fleeces that are woolier, thicker, and furrier than the typical two-sided fabrics.

Polarguard/Polarguard HV — High-loft, synthetic insulation of 100 percent polyester, continuous-filament fibres. Polarguard is one of the original and most durable synfills, although it is somewhat bulky when stuffed. The newer HV version uses hollowed fibres and is about 25 percent more stuffable, but it retains longevity.

Polartec — The family name for polyester fleece fabrics used by a variety of manufacturers. It comes in different weights for layering versatility; the Series 300 is heavyweight, double-sided fleece. A 300-series jacket is almost as warm as a down sweater but more versatile and virtually unaffected by water.

Polyester — Frequently blended with cotton, rayon, or other synthetics, this synthetic fibre features quick drying time, high strength, and resistance to abrasion and creasing.

Polypropylene — See *Olefin.*

Polyurethane coating — Polymer- or chemical-based waterproof coating applied to the inside of a fabric. In its heavy, waterproof, nonbreathable form, it is used in objects like tents and packs. In its lighter, microporous, breathable form, it is used in outerwear.

Primaloft — A high-loft synthetic insulation of large and small diameter polyester fibres intermingled to create a down-like feel and spring. Remarkably water resistant, this is a good choice for boaters and wet-weather hikers. Used in insulated clothing and sleeping bags.

Propile — A fuzzy nylon pile fabric, knitted so it will not pill like typical polyester pile.

Quallofil — A seven-channel Dacron polyester high-loft insulation with a soft, down-like feel. Used primarily in sleeping bags but also for insulated outerwear.

Rayon — The generic term for fibres derived from trees, cotton, and woody plants, it has a shiny appearance, dyes and drapes well, and feels silky, but it is too absorbent for good moisture management. Used mostly in base layers and trail clothing.

Ripstop — A fabric woven with double thread at regular intervals to achieve small squares that prevent tears from spreading. Usually applies to nylon or polyester. Found in outerwear, sleeping bags, packs, and tents.

Sixty-Forty — The 60 percent cotton/40 percent nylon fabric used in the classic "60/40" mountain parkas. It has reasonable water repellency but is not waterproof. It wears like iron yet exhibits a soft, cottony hand.

Taslan — An air-jet–textured nylon yarn used to create fabrics recognized for cottony feel, light weight, durability, and abrasion resistance; similar to Supplex (a fine-woven, quick-drying nylon) but coarser.

Thermal Dynamics — A 100 percent polyester base-layer fabric with differently textured inner and outer surfaces to move moisture out from skin. Used in underwear.

Thermastat — A fabric made from varying denier and staple length hollow-core polyester fibres; used in base-layer fabrics and, in theory, works as your body demands (cool when warm, warm when cool).

Thinsulate — A 35 percent polyester/65 percent olefin blend insulation spun into a low-loft construction. This is an efficient insulator considering its minimal thickness and is most often used in outerwear, footwear, and gloves because of its lack of bulk.

Tri-blend — Any fabric consisting of a blend of three fibres, frequently cotton/polyester/nylon or polyester/nylon/Lycra.

Tricot — A fabric knitted with two threads, it resists ravelling and tearing.

VBL — A vapour-barrier layer or liner, this is the generic name of a thin, plastic-like layer of clothing or socks that traps heat vapour in extremely cold conditions.

Wicking — The act of pulling moisture and sweat away from your skin and dispersing it throughout a material, a critical attribute in high-performance base layers.

Zendura — A 100 percent recycled pile fabric made from plastic soda bottles.

With some understanding of the jargon used by the textile industry, you should be able to select appropriate attire with greater confidence. Because clothing is your first line of defence against cold, it is vital to protect yourself with the best quality, most effective clothing available.

Footwear

Protecting your feet against the cold is no easy matter. Breathable footwear is preferable, and if your work or travel exposes you to water underfoot then special waterproof footwear is required.

ILLUSTRATION 36 — **Cold-Weather Footwear**

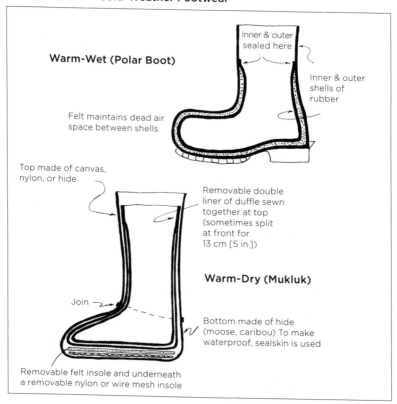

Warm-dry boots — First Nations people in North America have traditionally used moccasins or mukluks made from moose or caribou hide, which is hard to improve upon. The hide is hard-wearing and breathable, two of the qualities most needed for cold-weather use. Originally, grasses were used for insulation inside such footwear, but nowadays felt or duffel insoles of various thicknesses are common. A wire or plastic mesh insole between the felt and the bottom of the mukluk offers ventilation under the foot, and any moisture that does accumulate can be dried or, if ice has formed, beaten off. The most important thing to remember is that to be effective, the insulating layers must be kept as dry as possible. Nightly drying of moccasin and mukluk insulation is an important ritual of northern life.

Warm-wet boots — The alternative to the warm-dry type of footwear is the warm-wet boot that was first developed for military use in cold climates. This type of footwear relies on the vapour-barrier principle. The foot is literally encased in a hermetic environment. The "polar boot," as it is called, is in essence an inner rubber boot sealed inside a rubber outer shell. The space between the inner and outer boot is filled with felt in order to maintain an air space. The foot cannot breathe, so the wearer experiences a continual dampness created by perspiration, which cannot escape. The foot is moist but warm. This is a very effective type of footwear that requires no overnight drying and no other maintenance whatsoever. However, the boot is heavy, and if it were accidentally punctured you would have cold feet.

Other winter boots — There are many types of so called winter boots on the market. Many of these have rubber bottoms and leather or canvas tops. The effectiveness of such footwear will depend on your level of activity, whether they have built-in insulation at the bottom, and how dry you keep the insoles. The essential weakness comes from the fact that the rubber does not allow breathing, so perspiration builds up to impregnate the insoles. Your feet will get colder faster in this type of boot than they would if you had a moosehide mukluk.

Anyone who may be exposed to water in the course of their travels should carry a pair of light rubber overshoes that can be slipped over a moosehide moccasin or mukluk. The Inuit have traditionally used sealskin boots to provide protection from water.

If you are travelling on skis, wear high gaiters or an overboot. Skiers should also carry lightweight down or synthetically filled booties that offer protection when you are camped or sleeping. The body's extremities (including the feet) are the first to suffer the effects of cold, so pay attention to the efficiency of your footwear.

Protect Your Skin and Eyes

Severe sunburn can take place on a cloudy day. Sunburn and snow-blindness can have long-term consequences, so it is worth knowing when the risk is highest. Table 11 shows **albedo** (reflective power) values for various surfaces reflecting solar radiation will help in this respect.

TABLE 11 — **Reflective Power of Various Surfaces**

Surface	Albedo (%)
fresh snow cover	75-95
dense cloud cover	60-90
old snow cover	40-70
clean, firm snow	50-65
clean glacier ice and sea ice	30-46
desert	24-30
bare fields/tundra	12-25
forests	5-20
dark, cultivated soil	7-10
water (excluding large angles of incidence*)	3-10

Note: This table is reproduced by permission from *The Growth and Decay of Ice*, by G.S.H. Lock. *A "large angle of incidence" occurs when the sun is high above the horizon, resulting in a high angle of reflection.

FOOD ESSENTIALS

The first thing to say on the subject of food is that the priorities of the potential winter traveller are quite different from those of the typical North American urban dweller. Anyone exposed to the cold while hauling a sled or driving a snowmobile all day should select suitable nourishment on the basis of the following:

1. food energy (calories per kilogram or pound)
2. ease of preparation (depending on available cooking facilities and time)
3. preservation (influenced by temperature and duration of journey)
4. bulk and weight (depending on mode of travel)
5. taste

Table 12 shows the number of calories required to perform certain types of activity over and above that required for basal metabolism (the least amount of energy required by a body completely at rest). This table demonstrates that we must make considerable allowance

TABLE 12 — **Energy Expended above Basal Metabolism**

Activity	Calories per hour per 45 kg (100 lb) of body weight
eating	20
sitting quietly	20
walking 3 km/h (2 mph) on level pavement	80
driving an automobile	40
doing chores (fetching wood or water)	50
walking 4 km/h (3 mph) on level pavement	180
shivering	200–400
sawing wood	260
climbing	300–450
cross-country ski-touring	300

Note: Basal metabolism value is 1,100 large calories (kcal) per 45 kg (100 lb) of body weight per hour.

for exertion. No values have been given to take into account the extra calories needed to replace body-heat loss due to cold temperatures.

The calorie requirements given in Table 13 serve only as a general guide. The efficiency of the body in doing work over and above basal metabolism varies from 20 to 40 percent. Assuming an average value of 30 percent efficiency, the energy needed to raise 45 kilograms (100 pounds) at 305 metres (1,000 feet) of elevation is about 110 calories. Basal metabolism alone utilizes 1,100 calories per day per 45 kilograms (100 pounds) of body weight. This must be added to the activity calorie requirements given on the chart when calculating daily calorie requirements. The final factor in calculating energy requirements is the specific dynamic action (SDA). During digestion, 6 to 10 percent of the calorie content of food is released as heat, and thus is not available for basic metabolism or work. In extreme cold, the percentage lost to the production of heat is much higher.

TABLE 13 — **Calculating Energy Requirements**

Activity	Calories per hour	Duration of activity (hours)	Total calorie requirements
basal metabolism			1,870
eating	34	2	68
cross-country skiing	510	6	3,060
camp chores	85	2	170
subtotal			5,168
SDA 7%			362
total kcal			5,530

This example is based on a 77-kg (170-lb) person; hence basal metabolism is calculated as 1,100 x 1.7).

Food Values

Make every attempt to balance your menu with the correct proportions of carbohydrates, proteins, and fats. Most sources recommend a ratio of one protein to two fats to four carbohydrates, but for more concentrated diets it is closer to two proteins to three fats to four carbohydrates. Protein is a structural element for growth and repair, and fats and carbohydrates provide the fuel. Fats can be considered reserve energy, while carbohydrates provides quick energy and must be frequently replenished. The desire for fatty foods increases considerably when the body is exposed to cold temperatures. I can readily digest great dollops of butter when travelling and living for an extended period of time in a polar, or even subpolar, environment. I suppose one only has to observe the Inuit diet, which relies on high-fat seal meat, to find a parallel.

It helps to compare ration values used by various polar parties during travel and exploration of polar regions. Sledging rations providing 5,000 to 6,000 calories per day, with a ratio of 1 protein to 1.4 fat to 1.5 carbohydrate, were successful, whereas some other man-hauling rations providing more than 6,000 calories with a greater percentage of energy derived from fat were not quite as successful.

Nowadays there is a wide variety of conveniently packaged dehydrated and freeze-dried foodstuffs for load-conscious outdoor enthusiasts. Food companies offer complete freeze-dried meals sold in many outdoor equipment stores at a premium price, but I have always been able to find everything I need in the dehydrated food section of the supermarket. I have experimented with freeze-dried items, but have found the caloric value simply lacking. Table 14 shows the value of foodstuffs that can be used to constitute nutritious menus.

TABLE 14 — **Food Values**

Food (measure)	Water (%)	Energy (cal)	Protein (g)	Fat (g)	Carbs (g)
apricots, dried (1 cup, 250 mL)	25	390	8	1	100
beans, cooked (1 cup, 250 mL)	71	190	13	1	34
butter (½ cup, 125 mL)	16	810	1	92	1
cereal (oatmeal) (1 cup, 250 mL)	87	130	5	2	23
cheese (cheddar) (28 g, 1 oz)	37	115	7	9	1
chocolate, sweet (28 g, 1 oz)	1	145	2	9	16
cocoa, with milk (1 cup, 250 mL)	79	245	10	12	27
corned beef (85 g, 3 oz)	59	185	22	10	0
corned beef hash (85 g, 3 oz)	67	155	7	10	9
corn oil (1 tbsp, 25 mL)	0	125	0	14	0
dates, pitted (1 cup, 250 mL)	22	490	4	1	130
honey (1 tbsp, 25 mL)	17	65	0	0	17
macaroni, cooked (1 cup, 250 mL)	72	155	5	1	32
milk (dry skim) (1 cup, 250 mL)	4	245	24	0	35
peanuts (roasted, shelled halves) (1 cup, 250 mL)	2	840	37	72	27
peanut butter (1 tbsp, 25 mL)	2	95	4	8	3
peas (green, whole, dried) (1 cup, 250 mL)	70	290	20	1	52
pilot bread (1 biscuit)	30	100	2	5	13
potato, boiled in peel)	80	105	3	0	23
raisins (muscat, seeded) (1 cup, 250 mL)	18	480	4	0	28
rice (white, enriched, instant) (1 cup, 250 mL)	73	180	4	0	40

Food (measure)	Water (%)	Energy (cal)	Protein (g)	Fat (g)	Carbs (g)
sardines (85 g, 3 oz)	62	175	20	9	0
Snickers bar (61 g, 2 oz)	-	-	290	-	-
spaghetti (1 cup, 250 mL)	70	155	5	1	32
sugar (white, granulated) (1 cup, 250 mL)	0	770	0	0	199
tuna (canned in oil, drained solids) (1 cup, 250 mL)	61	170	24	7	0
whole wheat bread (1 slice)	36	65	3	1	14

Ease of Preparation

Traditionally, winter travellers have, for several obvious reasons, relied on menus and meals that could be prepared in a single pot. All manner of ingredients have been included in **hooshes** to provide a high-calorie product that provides the right proportion of protein, fat, and carbohydrates. Nowadays we have a good idea of what foods (combined with vitamin supplements) are required for a specific activity in a specific environment.

Snacks

We all have our preferences, but here is a list of my favourite snack foods:

- fruit cake or Logan bread (see recipe on page 127)
- bannock with jam spread (see recipe on page 126)
- pilot bread with butter and cheese
- peanut or almond butter and honey sandwiches
- Snickers
- dates
- hard candies (the best quality)
- dried apricots

Winter Trail Cooking Kit

For adventurous outdoor enthusiasts who are planning treks of several days' duration, a winter trail cooking kit will prove invaluable. The major advantage of this design is that it can melt snow or ice at the same time as it cooks a meal. The metal shield, or skirt, attached to the melt pot serves both as a heat retainer and a windshield.

Basically, a snow/ice melt pot is attached (press-fitted or riveted) to a cylindrical tube (shield). The bottom of this pot serves as the lid to the shielded cooking pot. My own shield was made from a 4.54-litre (160–fluid ounce) paint can with both ends removed, which fortuitously accommodated one of my stainless steel camp pots. I needed only to press-fit the pot into one end, allowing for 160 holes of 9 millimetres (⅜ inch) diameter to be drilled in the lower portion of the shield, up to a point in line with the bottom of the melt pot.

TRADITIONAL TRAIL BANNOCK
(Yields two bannocks or six to eight servings)

3 cups (625 mL) all-purpose or
   whole wheat flour
2 tbsp (30 mL) baking powder
½ tsp (2 mL) salt
2 tbsp (30 mL) sugar
¼ cup (59 mL) butter
1 cup (250 mL) water
raisins, currants, or berries
   (optional)

Combine flour, baking powder, salt and sugar in basin, along with (optional) raisins, currants, or berries. Add butter; rub in to form fine crumbs. Add water and stir to form soft dough, kneading for 10 seconds.

Lightly grease a heavy skillet with butter.

Dust the bannock dough with flour and place half of the dough in the skillet (the remaining half can be used for seconds on the following day). Heat over live coals for 5 minutes. Raise pan to 45 centimetres (18 inches) above coals and bake for 5 to 10 minutes or until underside of the dough is brown and crusty.

Cool and serve, adding a topping of butter, jam, or maple syrup as desired.

MONTY'S LOGAN BREAD*

(*This bread is made before you set out on your trip.)

Preheat oven to 163°C (325°F).

Grease 4 medium (10 x 20 cm, 4 x 8 inch) baking tins, 8 small (7 x 15 cm, 3 x 5 inch) mini-loaf tins, or one 23 x 33 cm (9 x 13 inch) pan plus one 23 x 23 cm (9 inch x 9 inch) pan.

In a very large bowl, measure and mix together the following dry ingredients:

3 cups (750 mL) whole wheat flour
1 cup (250 mL) brown sugar
1 cup (250 mL) quick oats
½ cup (125 mL) unsulphured raisins
½ cup (125 mL) dried apricots, chopped
½ cup (125 mL) dried cranberries
1 cup (250 mL) pitted dates, chopped
½ cup (125 mL) walnuts or pecans, toasted and chopped
¼ cup (60 mL) wheat germ
½ cup (125 mL) sesame seeds
1 tbsp (15 mL) baking powder
¼ tsp (1 mL) salt
½ tsp (2.5 mL) nutmeg

In another large bowl, mix together the following wet ingredients:

½ cup (125 mL) vegetable oil
½ cup (125 mL) blackstrap molasses
1 cup (250 mL) applesauce
½ cup (125 mL) water
1 cup (250 mL) liquid honey
½ cup (125 mL) milk
3 eggs

Pour the wet ingredients into the dry ingredients, mixing until well blended. Portion the batter into the prepared pans, filling each about ⅔ full. Put any extra batter into well-greased ramekins. (These will look dense and travel well, if individually wrapped.)

Bake in preheated oven for about 1 hour and 15 minutes for larger loaf tins, 45 minutes for smaller tins, and 30 minutes for ramekins. Test with toothpick or skewer, and when it comes out clean, it is done.

Leave to cool on a rack for 15 minutes, then remove from tins. Let cool completely before wrapping or slicing.

The actual cooking pot (smaller than the melt pot) is set on the stove and the shield/melt pot set on top, so the bottom of the melt pot not only serves as a lid, but also collects heat to melt snow or ice.

The height of a lightweight stove (in this case a Peak 1) keeps the shield clear of the ground to allow ample draft. The stove is recessed into a wood base that doubles as the bottom cover when the kit is packed for travel. The varnished plywood top and bottom covers are joined by a strap. While the stove must be packed separately, the cook pot can be packed inside the melt pot, and other cooking utensils or food can be stowed in the space under the melt pot.

Two configurations can be used:

1. Stove directly under the larger melt pot
2. Stove, cook pot and melt pot (as illustrated on page 129)

When using an open-flame gas stove in an enclosed area, take care to ensure that there is adequate ventilation, and be particularly careful when melting snow. An efficient open-flame camp stove burns with a blue flame that is very hot, far above 1,000°C (1,832°F). In such a flame, the

A suggested trail stove.

combustion is complete, so the fuel is converted to safe carbon dioxide (CO_2). However, if the flame is cooled by a cold object (like the bottom of a pan containing snow or ice) and shows a yellow colour, then combustion is incomplete, resulting in the release of deadly carbon monoxide.

ILLUSTRATION 37 — **Northern Trail Cooker**

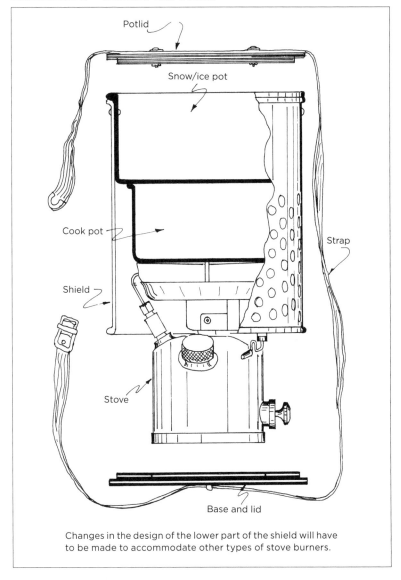

Potlid

Snow/ice pot

Cook pot

Strap

Shield

Stove

Base and lid

Changes in the design of the lower part of the shield will have to be made to accommodate other types of stove burners.

The view of the entrance to an igloo from the inside.

chapter 7

~

A SURVIVAL SCENARIO

THIS COULD HAPPEN TO YOU

IT WAS A LOVELY winter afternoon with the low, not warm, but dazzling sun giving long shadows to every object protruding above the surface of the snow. The temperature was just snappy enough to make our Sunday ski jaunt exhilarating. My companion, Joan, and I were following a skidoo track above the treeline to the southeast of Golden Horn Mountain. Whoever had packed the snow with their machine had not done so with cross-country skiers in mind. There were many sharp rises and too many sharper dips. It was while negotiating a particularly deep impression that Joan failed to negotiate the sharp turn at the bottom and, hitting a boulder sticking out of the snow, broke one of her skis and severely sprained her ankle.

The pain it gave her made the two-hour trip back to the road, where our vehicle was parked, completely out of the question. Fortunately, two of our closest friends, with whom we shared lodgings, were well aware of our plans and knew exactly where we were going. But while we could rest assured they would begin to organize a search as soon as we failed to show for supper, we could hardly expect this to take place after dark. Unless a snow machine happened to come by in the next two hours, we would simply have to stay put overnight.

Apart from having shared our plans with others, we had both had the foresight to include personal survival kits in our day packs. Mine had been borrowed and was not as complete as Joan's. We also had a few spare items of clothing and the remains of lunch. I had spare socks that could be used as mitts, a sweater, a scarf, two large garbage bags, half a cheese sandwich (frozen), and a bag of mixed nuts and raisins.

Unfortunately, the site offered little in the way of visible firewood, so we had no choice but to make the best out of what our kits contained and what the snow and vegetation promised in the way of shelter. Although I had not taken the survival course offered by the Outdoor Club, my roommate had and it was she who had impressed upon both of Joan and I the value of an emergency kit. She had also shown us slides of the various snow houses the class had constructed. As enthusiastic skiers and lovers of the outdoors we had both read books on the subject of winter survival, which emphasized the importance of building as good a shelter as time, circumstance, and available materials allowed.

Poor Joan couldn't move much without feeling a great deal of pain. Her left ankle had swollen considerably. She had donned the spare clothing contained in her day pack, and I made a pad of sticks and vegetation for her to sit on, well insulated from the snow. What she was able to do while I began shelter construction was activate her survival kit and start melting snow using the candle stove it contained. We were lucky that there was no wind.

We were also fortunate that we had found a drift with snow of sufficient depth and density to favour the construction of a simple snow trench, which has the advantage of keeping you dry during construction. Having wet clothing, either externally from contact with snow or internally from sweating, is certainly not the way to begin a night in a subpolar environment. Using the tail end of Joan's broken ski as a shovel, and then as a chisel to pry blocks loose for a roof, our shelter took shape. Of course, it would have been much quicker and easier if I had had a shovel and a snow saw—a lesson learned! Not remembering the finer details of roof construction, like a key to prevent the toe of the roof block from moving, I finally managed to peak-roof the trench that I had excavated. Simple as the shelter was, I was surprised to find that it had taken me a good hour and a half, and it was now already dusk. Joan had by that time melted enough snow—an equally time-consuming process—for us to enjoy a mug (can) of warm water flavoured with a melted chocolate bar. The brew was not as hot as we would have liked, but it gave us both an immense lift—in both the physiological and psychological sense of the word. It made us feel that we had everything under control.

Collecting sufficient bush tops to make an insulating pad (bed) inside the shelter absorbed another hour so that by the time I had blocked in the ends and cut the smallest entry hole it was completely dark. We combined what odds and ends we had in one day pack and used the other to cover the entrance.

We were both surprised how cozy it was inside with two candles burning under two cans to provide more water. The same candles provided light and some warmth. Our body heat also warmed the shelter so that, lying on a good thickness of brush, with the lower part of our bodies inside the garbage bags and wearing all our extra clothing we were not uncomfortably cold. The temperature outside was −20°C (−4°F), according to the small zipper-pull thermometer on my ski jacket, and inside it was around 0°C (32°F).

I was just dozing off when Joan said, "It just occurred to me that if someone comes looking for us they might not see the shelter." It was a good point, since we occupied a drift that was a short distance east of the track. I had stuck my skis in the snow by the side of the trail but agreed that we should try to make the site as conspicuous as possible.

I tied a large red handkerchief to a bush that flanked the track and placed Joan's broken ski in the middle of the trail.

At 9:00 p.m. we made a brew of Oxo using a cube that I found at the bottom of my day pack left over from an earlier foray. At midnight we shared the half cheese sandwich dunked in another cup of brew. As we ate and drank, I changed the cold, snow-wetted bandage around Joan's ankle. If there was one thing I knew, it was how easy it was to become dehydrated and that such a condition could pave the way to hypothermia.

As I lay there, curled up close to Joan, it occurred to me how serious this situation would have been had I been alone and hit a tree. Could I have built the shelter standing on one leg? I realized that the oft-repeated advice to always travel in pairs was no idle suggestion. With the almost constant need to replenish the cook pot with snow, keep Joan's ankle cold and replace the candles, the night passed quicker than either of us expected. By early morning we had gone through twelve tea lights and had consumed several cans of warm beverages.

The shelter had served us well. It had reduced heat loss through radiation, as had the garbage bags, which acted like vapour barriers; it had prevented body heat being carried away by convection; loss of heat through exercise and sweating had been minimal, and because the air temperature inside was 20°C (68°F) warmer than outside the loss of heat through respiration had been reduced considerably. Finally, the scraps of vegetation beneath us prevented loss of heat through conduction.

We were perhaps as close to being asleep as we had been all night when we heard the much muted whine of a snow machine. We placed Joan on the sled inside the sleeping bag that had been brought along, and we were both grateful for the hot Thermos of tea that was thrust in our hands. It wasn't long before we reached the road, the warm trucks, and the embraces of our friends.

It was a happy ending to a relatively minor accident that could happen to anyone, an incident that nonetheless could have been far more life-threatening had we not had some knowledge of survival techniques and been equipped with personal survival kits. One thing we did know is that we would never go anywhere, even for a day, without letting someone know exactly where we were going and the time we expected to return. On top of that, we would never go anywhere in winter without a PSK and some tools to facilitate the construction of a snow shelter.

Survival Tips

* Leave a detailed itinerary with a responsible person or agency.

* Always remember the value of shelter and know how to utilize available materials such as vegetation and snow.

* Understand how the body reacts to cold, and watch for signs of frostbite and hypothermia.

* Remember to stay hydrated and have with you the means to make a warm beverage.

* Bring appropriate provisions and understand the value of high-calorie, quick-acting snack foods.

* Remember to bring fire starters, but also know that enclosed shelters that utilize the insulating properties of snow offer greater protection from cold.

* Stay positive.

SIGNALS

In the search for an overdue person or party, the efficiency of the search will largely depend on the amount of detail the traveller has left behind with reliable contacts. If you have clearly indicated your route on a map, the chances of being rescued in a timely fashion are much better. However, if you do find yourself lost, knowing how to attract the attention of a search party is paramount.

Making conspicuous physical changes to your place of confinement will make it more visible to both land and air search parties. There are a number of things that you can do to make your site stand out. Spreading a coloured panel (blue, orange, or black if your surroundings are predominantly white) may catch the eye of a search aircraft. Or you can make a **lobstick** by de-limbing an isolated tree so that only the top remains fully branched, creating an attention-grabbing anomaly. If you have any reflecting material, drape it over a bush. Anything you can do to disfigure the landscape will prompt a second glance by a search observer.

If you are marooned with a vehicle or aircraft, it is important to keep it snow-free so that it will remain visible.

In addition to the above there are a number of specific, internationally recognized distress signals that could be prepared or laid out on the ground.

International Distress Signals

Fire — Three fires in a triangle of 30-metre (100-foot) sides or in a straight line 30 metres (100 feet) apart. These should be ready for firing as soon as you hear an aircraft. Build the fires so they produce smoke during the day and flame during the night.

S.O.S. — Tramp the letters in snow and fill the depressions with boughs. This should be done in a large exposed area. You can also tramp out the internationally accepted ground-to-air code (see page 137). If there is no snow on the ground, use stones or vegetation to make appropriate signs. Each arm should be 1 metre (3 feet) wide and 10 metres (33 feet) long. Such depressions or mounds should be oriented north to south to create shadows.

Morse code — Use a flashlight to flash S.O.S. in Morse code (three short flashes followed by three long and three short flashes).

Gun shots or whistle blasts — Three gun shots, or whistle blasts, at 10-second intervals is a distress signal. A ground party would reply with two shots.

TABLE 15 — **Ground-to-Air Emergency Code**

International	Canada Only
V	LL
Require Assistance	All is Well
X	F
Require Medical Assistance	Require Food and Water
N	L
No	Require Fuel and Oil
Y	W
Yes	Require Repairs
↑	Note: arms of letters must be 10 m (33 ft.) long and 1 m (3 ft.) wide.
Proceeding in This Direction	

You Are Not Alone When You Have a Phone

All cell phones operate within a network of relay beacons, or towers, so when you know that you are likely to travel beyond the reaches to these beacons, you must consider other means of contacting others.

VHF (Very High Frequency) Transceivers — I have used a small hand-held transceiver to great advantage when travelling within sight of appropriate microwave towers. Such transmissions have allowed me to contact a network operator who can connect me with the number I wish to reach.

Satellite Phones — Recently, when exploring southeastern Alaska by sailboat, I used an Iridium satellite phone. These phones are a little larger than a VHF hand-held transceiver but still compact enough to carry in a small shoulder bag. The downside of satellite phones is that they are expensive to buy and have costly access fees and calling charges. However, you can rent a satellite phone for the duration of your journey and use it just for emergencies or to contact your loved ones at home to report that all is well.

SPOT Personal Tracker — At the press of a button, this very compact and inexpensive device can automatically transmit the coordinates of your location as well as a pre-programmed message to a specific security base or your home. It does not transmit speech, but as an economical safety device, it is worth considering.

Carrying a communication device that will dispel your concerns and can be used in an emergency could not only save a life but also be of valuable assistance to a rescue team. Always check with a reputable electronics communications company to see what is currently available. Like a lot of electronic equipment, new designs are continuously coming on the market. For those who travel in winter off the main highways, including reliable communication equipment in your kit is of paramount importance.

Other Means of Signalling

Mirror — Be sure you know how to aim the mirror using a finger as a foresight (see pages 140).

Flares — Keep a pocket or pencil flare gun in your PSK. Use red flares during the day and white flares at night.

Flashes — Use flint and steel at night to create a bright flash.

Signal Mirrors

Anything shiny can be used to reflect sunlight—even a piece of ice. Signal mirrors of different sizes, with various design features built in to facilitate sighting them, can be purchased at most outdoor equipment stores.

The purpose of the signal mirror is to attract the attention of a search party by reflecting the rays of the sun (from whatever azimuth the sun may be in at the time) in the direction of a ground or air search party. It is possible to do this through an arc of just over 120 degrees.

In order to accomplish this using a variety of reflective materials (including ice) with no built-in

ILLUSTRATION 38 —

VHF Hand-held Transceiver

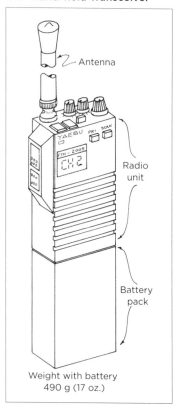

Antenna

Radio unit

Battery pack

Weight with battery
490 g (17 oz.)

sighting device, you should be aware of a sighting trick. The secret, for a right-handed person, is to point a finger of an extended left hand at the search party, or aircraft, and then, with the mirror held between the finger and thumb of your right hand a few centimetres from your dominant eye, tilt the mirror until you illuminate your extended finger. It helps to first produce a spot on the ground in front of you and then slowly move it to the finger. When this is accomplished, and the finger remains pointed at the search team, you can be sure that they will see the mirror's reflection.

ILLUSTRATION 39 — **Signalling mirror**

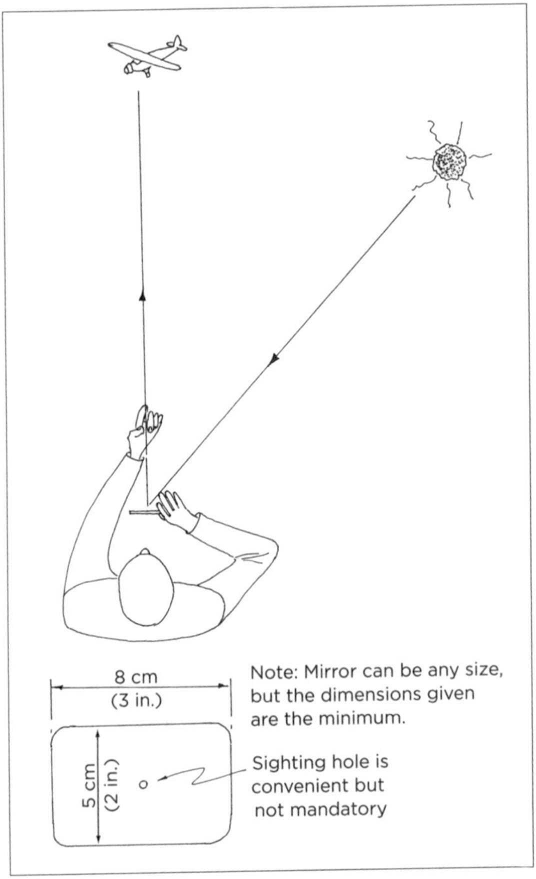

8 cm
(3 in.)

5 cm
(2 in.)

Note: Mirror can be any size, but the dimensions given are the minimum.

Sighting hole is convenient but not mandatory

FIRES

We have considered the reaction of the human body to cold and how to use ice and snow for travel and survival. We have considered clothing as the first line of defence against cold, to prevent body-heat loss. Now it is time to give thought to those things that provide heat, and what to include in your PSK.

Knowing how to light a fire using whatever materials may be available is essential. Most of us believe that lighting a fire in the woods takes little expertise and would be no problem at all providing we have a box of matches or a pocket lighter. This may be true in the heat of summer, when a carelessly thrown cigarette butt can start a forest fire, but to get a fire going in winter, especially in sub-zero temperatures, is another matter entirely. Small sticks suitable for kindling that will ignite so readily in summer defy combustion in winter since they often contain ice crystals that are invisible to the eye and that melt when a match is applied. Further handicaps, such as numb fingers and hands and matches that break easily makes fire lighting a process that requires care, patience, and a little skill. The key is to have with you an effective **fire starter.**

A fire consists of four parts:
1. starter (inflammable items, including tinder)
2. kindling (very small sticks)
3. primary fuel (larger sticks)
4. final fuel (dry logs)

To facilitate combustion any fire must have adequate oxygen, and all fuel should be as dry as possible. The arrangement of kindling is important. Some people use a traditional pyramid construction, while others prefer a cross-stick pattern. The objective is to allow air to reach the fire.

Site selection is also important. Never build a fire under a snow-laden tree, and if there is deep snow then either clear it away to bare ground or build your fire on a platform of green wood. Whatever the construction method a good supply of kindling and fuel must be gathered before you strike the first match or apply steel to flint.

Before you set out on a trip, I strongly recommend that you practise using various starters under a variety of conditions. And remember that just because there is snow on the ground doesn't mean you can leave the site of the fire without making absolutely sure it is out. A forest floor of moss and humus can smolder for a long time and be fanned into flame by wind long after the snow cover has gone.

Recommended Fire Starters Used with Matches

- toilet tissue
- a piece of waxed paper, 30 centimetres (12 inches) square
- two rubber bands (the thick type used to hold together vegetables such as broccoli) wrapped around a box of waterproof matches
- fire paste (sold in a tube at hardware and outdoor sports shops; carry in a waterproof bag)
- waxed lamp wick (buy a strip of lamp wick, dip it in melted parawax, then cut it in 5-centimetre, or 2-inch lengths)
- duct tape
- felt from felt marker pen
- candle
- boot conditioner (Aquaseal or Sno-Seal)
- commercial fire starters (available in hardware stores in stick form)
- Coffee-Mate
- Band-Aids
- a small, tight-lidded container filled with sawdust that is saturated with kerosene or diesel
- inner bark of dead trees that can be fluffed between palms to provide excellent tinder

Recommended Fire Starters Used with Flint and Steel

- extra-fine steel wool, grade 0000 (squeeze a little fire paste on top to prolong flame and blow on it to energize the flame)
- cotton wool (impregnate with fire paste)
- model airplane glue (Testors)
- vinyl mender (Devcon)
- vinyl plastic repair (LePage)
- powder from ammunition (break open a cartridge and pour gunpowder on tinder)

Other Possibilities

- using camera or binocular lens to focus sunlight on a starter or tinder
- creating friction with a bow drill (requires considerable practice)
- using a 9-volt battery to ignite steel wool, with fire paste imbedded (see illustration below)

ILLUSTRATION 40 — **An Alternative Fire Starter**

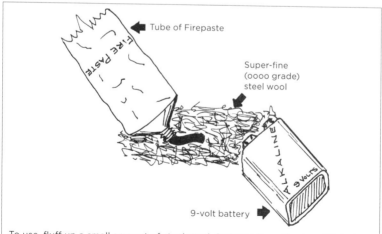

Tube of Firepaste

Super-fine (0000 grade) steel wool

9-volt battery

To use, fluff up a small amount of steel wool. Squeeze 3 centimetres (1⅛ inches) of paste atop the wool. Apply the terminals of a 9-volt battery to the pad of wool. As soon as a glow appears, blow on it to increase the burn until the paste is ignited. Apply wood kindling.

- mixing potassium permanganate from a first-aid kit and glycol from radiator (½ teaspoon, 2 mL, potassium to nine drops glycol) is self-igniting
- vehicle cigarette lighter
- sparking of vehicle battery with leads held in sensitive tinder
- Bic (or equivalent brand) lighter (does not function too well in cold)

Fire Tips

- A toilet-paper roll, rolled-up corrugated paper, or dried moss, when placed in a coffee or tobacco can and soaked with either methyl hydrate, diesel, kerosene, animal fat, or fish fat will serve as a portable burner (heater) for several hours.
- Vehicle or aircraft tires burn well but you need a fire to initiate burning.
- Dry animal droppings have been used as fire material for centuries.
- If using a wood fire, feed it. Do not waste time and energy cutting up wood; simply place one end of a large stick or log into the fire, and as it burns, keep feeding the remainder.
- If you fill an egg carton with lint from a clothes dryer, then pour in parawax, you will have twelve fire starters.
- Jack pine and lodgepole pine provide good kindling.
- Tamarack (larch) provides good heat with few sparks.
- Willow offers a good fire with the least smoke.
- Smoke from white spruce is irritating to the eyes and lungs.
- Black spruce is the easiest to limb from the top down.
- Black poplar is the poorest of firewood.
- Aspen offers a good blaze and pleasant smoke.

MOTHER NATURE'S SURVIVAL FOOD

In a survival situation, you do not require food as much as you need water. Many people have survived extended periods without food—one downed airman spent fifty-two days without food before being rescued—but not without water. However, if you do end up in a situation where you have to look for food, note that procuring food from the wilderness is not so easy in winter if you are not trained to do so. The following sections describe food materials that are generally close at hand and easy to gather.

Plants

Kinnikinnick *(Arctostaphylos uva-ursi)* — also called bearberry, sandberry, and mealberry, this is a mat-like trailing shrub often found beneath the snow. The leaves are oval, thick, and leathery, and the flowers are pale pink in small terminal racemes. The berries are orangey-red and dry and mealy with seeds. The berries can be eaten as they are (rather tasteless), added to soups, or boiled and then fried in grease and sugar. They are rich in vitamin C and carbohydrates. The leaves can be used to make tea (two to three spoonfuls per cup). In Russia the resulting brew is called *kutai,* or Caucasian tea. Trappers and prospectors recommend soaking the leaves in whisky first (which sounds like a great idea, but whether it is beneficial against cold is questionable).

ILLUSTRATION 41 — **Kinnikinnick**

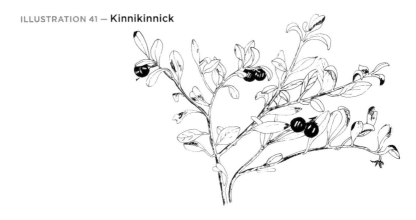

ILLUSTRATION 42 —

Labrador Tea

Labrador tea *(Ledum decumbens and a similar species Ledum groenlandicum)* — Also found under the snow cover, this evergreen shrub grows from 30 to 90 centimetres (12 to 36 inches) in height. The twigs are densely covered with wool. The alternate entire leaves are oblong in outline, blunt or rounded at the end with the margins rolled in. They are 2.5 to 5 centimetres (1 to 2 inches) long, dark green above, and densely covered with light brown wool beneath. The foliage is quite thick and leathery, and it is fragrant when crushed in the hand. The flowers, which appear in early summer, are on the ends of the twigs in short, umbel-like clusters. The numerous blossoms, less than 1 centimetre (0.5 inch), are white with five spreading petals. The small calyx is five-toothed. There are usually five stamens and a five-celled seedpod.

Leaves can be used for tea, though it is best to dry them first. Beware that Labrador tea does contain a poisonous compound called andromedotoxin that can cause headaches, cramps, and even paralysis if taken in excessive amounts. Steep one heaping spoonful of leaves, or flowers, per person in boiling water for 5 minutes. Do not steep longer.

Lodgepole pine *(Pinus contorta)* — The egg-shaped cones are small, 3 to 5 centimetres (1 to 2 inches) in length, with prickly pointed scales often borne in clusters. Needles grow to 8 centimetres (3 inches) long in bunches of two or three, yellow or dark green.

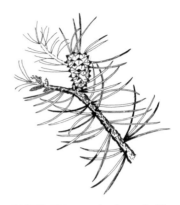

ILLUSTRATION 43 — **Lodgepole Pine**

The needles make a pleasant, mild-tasting tea. Spruce, fir, and pine needles all make good tea, but again, use in moderation. In the spring the juicy inner bark (cambium) can be eaten fresh or dried. In the dry state it can be used as an emergency food, boiled or added to stews. The seeds are also edible.

Wild Rose *(Rosa woodsii)* — Also called wood rose, this erect shrub grows to be 50 to 150 centimetres (20 to 59 inches) tall, and usually has thorny stems and seven to nine broadly ovate toothed leaflets. Flowers are usually solitary, pink, and showy. The frozen hips can be found hanging on the bushes in winter.

ILLUSTRATION 44 — **Wild Rose**

To make tea, use about ten to twelve hips per cup. You may crush, but not open, the hips (the bristly centres are mildly toxic) or use the husks with seeds and fibres removed. Steep in boiling water.

Fish

The most likely possibility for a more substantial food supply comes from the water. In winter, this imposes the need for ice-cutting tools or open water at rapids, lake outlets, at a shallow narrows in a lake, or someplace where there is a polynya. For a lure, all you need is a hook baited with a piece of reflecting or coloured, material. A commercial lure like a Red Devil also works. If you have to cut a hole in the ice, look for a spot where you can imagine a back eddy in summer.

An item that could be included in any survival kit without fear of weight or space is a gill net. A 1 x 6 metre (3 x 20 foot) nylon net with a mesh of 6 centimetres (2.5 inches) would allow you to catch small fish. It has been suggested that two nets of 3 metres (10 feet) long

ILLUSTRATION 45 — **Gill Net Set under Ice**

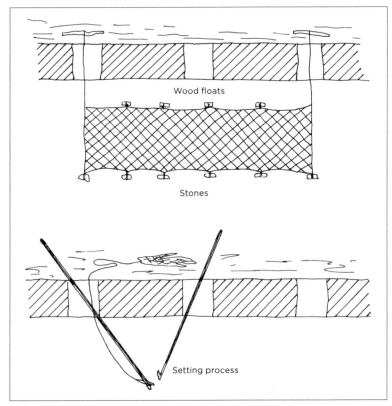

Wood floats

Stones

Setting process

and of different mesh size joined together lengthways—for example, one section with a 6-centimetre (2.5-inch) mesh and the other with a 9-centimetre (3.5-inch) mesh—is more efficient. Like the snare, a gill net can be catching food while you sleep.

Mammals and Birds

Rabbits and squirrels make visible runways in the snow, and a simple snare can be set either in the runway or, in the case of squirrels, on a pole leaning against a tree that they are using.

Last but certainly not least is the possibility that you will encounter grouse or ptarmigan. Native peoples have traditionally killed these with sticks, stones, and bows using a blunt arrow. Others have succeeded using a long pole with a snare at the end.

ILLUSTRATION 46 —
Snare for Rabbit

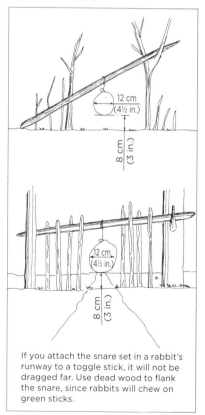

12 cm (4½ in.)

8 cm (3 in.)

12 cm (4½ in.)

8 cm (3 in.)

If you attach the snare set in a rabbit's runway to a toggle stick, it will not be dragged far. Use dead wood to flank the snare, since rabbits will chew on green sticks.

chapter 8

FALL

ILLUSTRATION 47 — **Lean-to**

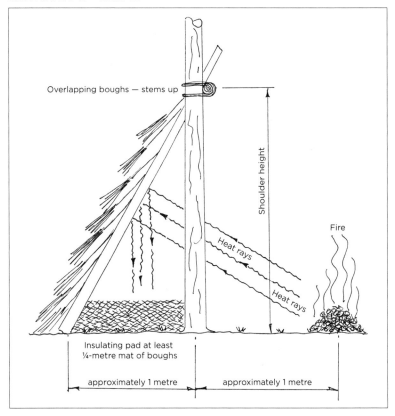

Overlapping boughs — stems up

Shoulder height

Heat rays

Heat rays

Fire

Insulating pad at least
¼-metre mat of boughs

approximately 1 metre

approximately 1 metre

WHILE THE FOCUS OF this manual is travel during winter, when snow and ice blanket the land, it is in that short period 'twixt summer and winter that we have to be especially careful. In the fall we can expect rain, snow flurries, a lot of wind, and cold temperatures that will awaken us to the fact that winter is around the corner. The danger lies in the fact that we are used to summer and, physiologically and psychologically, we are still unprepared for a hostile environment. We are more likely to be under-dressed and generally under-equipped for what nature can throw at us.

Since fall is when so many of us are either hunting, fishing, wood cutting, or getting in that last canoe trip, any suggestions for staying warm are pertinent. Most people, especially those who have had only fleeting experience in the outdoors, regard the mid-winter –20°C to –40°C (–4°F to –40°F) days as the ones demanding the greatest care. In actual fact, it is easier to combat a truly polar environment than one that is damp, cold, and windy. It is much easier to dress for a bitterly cold but dry climate than it is for a wet one. Clothing that is effective in keeping the rain out, like oilskins, is likely to trap in body moisture, especially if you are engaging in strenuous exercise. Fortunately, there are garments made of materials like Gore-Tex that will allow body moisture to escape and still provide rain protection.

In the fall, our hands and face are unaccustomed to cold, but by the end of winter, we are able to do all manner of things in cold temperatures that we could not have done at the beginning of the cold season. Similarly, we are less likely to be mentally prepared for cold at the beginning of fall as we are at the end. For example, we may forget to include a good fire starter in our kit that will enable us light a fire with wet wood. Or we may not thinking about that the combined effect of wet and wind and how these factors can easily lead to hypothermia.

In late fall, particularly in the more northern latitudes, rivers and lakes begin to freeze over. We have surfaces of newly formed ice that offer a tantalizing surface for the wilderness traveller. At this time, you need to know more about ice than the fact that it cools your drinks! Review the section on the relationship between ice thickness and bearing strength and equip yourself with a tool that measures ice thickness for your own safety.

A boating mishap in the fall is more likely to end in tragedy simply because the water temperature is colder than at the height of summer. A person becomes hypothermic very quickly. Our survival time in cold water depends on our body fat and how we are clothed, but in any case it is not long. On a lake the shore may look invitingly close, but your chances of reaching it by swimming in cold water are remote indeed.

Fall may offer many delights, absence of bugs, dazzling colours, and reduced danger of forest fires, but travelling during this time is only safe if we are adequately prepared for the worst possible autumnal weather that could be expected in a particular region.

SUMMARY: RULES FOR SURVIVAL

In order to emerge with a smile on your face from an enforced overnight in the wilderness in extremely cold temperatures, without the benefit of a sleeping bag or the heat of a fire, you must observe certain fundamental rules. The following recommendations constitute a summary of what has been suggested in various sections of this handbook.

Use the mnemonic KNACK to remind yourself of the following five things:

Knowledge. Be aware of the fundamentals of survival. Learn from reading, take a survival course, or accompanying someone who is more experienced on a winter wilderness trip.

Notification. Ensure that you leave as detailed an itinerary as possible with a responsible person or authority. Doing this will ensure that your time in the wilderness is more likely to be a brief one.

Attitude. Be confident and always project a positive attitude. This will help both you and your companion(s).

Clothing. Take with you enough of the right kind of clothing to afford protection in the worst weather that could be expected at that time of year in that location.

Kit. Be sure that you have a PSK and day pack with you whenever you leave a populated area to enter an isolated and predominantly cold environment.

Finally, be familiar with such survival techniques as shelter building, fire lighting, and signalling. Go slow, go safe, and enjoy the many wonders of winter.

~

A REFERENCE FOR TRAVELLERS

VEHICLE GUIDE

1. Do **not** carry your sleeping bag in the trunk, where the vehicle is coldest and where you could not get at it if the trunk were damaged or jammed.

2. If stranded, use your vehicle as a temporary refuge while you build a snow shelter. If the motor is operable, use the heater to dry any damp clothing. When the engine is running, be sure to have the window open a crack to alleviate any chance of carbon monoxide buildup.

3. Any non-running vehicle is a heat sink, offering no insulation from the cold.

4. Be sure to make your snow shelter visible from the road where your vehicle is stranded.

5. Vehicle seats and cushions offer good insulating pads for the inside of a snow shelter.

6. Tires will serve as emergency fuel for a fire. If it becomes necessary to burn them, it is best to add tires to an existing (already burning) wood fire.

7. A cigarette lighter can be used to ignite a fire starter.
8. The battery can be sparked to ignite a fire starter.
9. Flashing of headlights could guide a night-search aircraft.
10. Do not abandon your vehicle to walk along the road unless you can see a distant light suggesting habitation a few kilometres away, you are well clothed, the road is not subject to drifting snow, and its edges are visible. It is safer to hole up and wait for someone to find you, and how long you wait will depend on how detailed an itinerary you left with a responsible person prior to your departure. If you must leave your vehicle, make sure to leave a note telling search parties what direction you are taking and the time you left.
11. Do not allow snow to bury the vehicle. An all-white vehicle is a handicap. A blue vehicle stands out well because few things in the natural world are that colour.
12. Should you not have a signal mirror in your survival kit, try using a vehicle mirror to attract the attention of a search aircraft during a sunny day.
13. If you have an electronic means of communication such as a VHF transceiver, personal locator beacon, cell phone, or satellite phone, use it report your situation and give your location. If a member of your party is injured, make sure to call for a medic.

Vehicle Kit

Make sure your vehicle is equipped with the following items:
- PSK
- snow shovel
- axe
- flashlight with alkaline or lithium batteries
- tarpaulin big enough to cover engine hood and reach the ground on both sides

- spare fan belt
- spare fuses
- wheel wrench (preferably star type)
- battery jumper cables (with card showing correct hook-up procedure)
- extra spare wheel if driving along an isolated and unserviced highway
- tow chain and "jack-all," which in combination can be used as a come-along (a device offering a mechanical advantage when moving or towing)
- garbage bags (preferably large and blue), which can be used as an emergency shelter roof, snow shelter entrance cover, vapour-barrier clothing, or signal panel
- Thermos (kept topped up with hot, sweet drink)
- first-aid kit (including cushioned mask such as Airway SealEasy, used for sanitary purposes when administering CPR)
- sleeping bag (of winter weight and kept in cab rather than trunk)
- emergency heater (preferably gasoline camp stove and 2 metres, 6 feet, of 10-centimetre, 4-inch, stovepipe with two right-angle elbows, or alternatively a roll of kerosene- or diesel-soaked toilet paper inside a coffee)
- ban ice (methyl hydrate)
- antifreeze
- window scraper
- starting fluid
- several long-burning candles (at least 12 hours' combined burn time)
- tool kit (with a minimum of a screwdriver, adjustable wrench, and pliers)
- matches and striker (wood type) or flint and steel

- light lashing cord (50 metres, 165 feet)
- extra clothing and footwear
- road flares
- winter tires (check air pressure before departing)
- insulated pad (for use inside emergency shelter)
- at least two 10 x 10 x 30 centimetre (4 x 4 x 12 inch) wooden blocks

SNOWMOBILE GUIDE

1. Always travel in pairs (on separate machines).
2. If stranded, it is better to hole up in a snow shelter than to try to walk out. How long you have to wait for rescue will depend on how detailed the itinerary you left with a responsible person was.
3. Your discomfort, or your safety, will depend on how familiar you are with survival techniques and how fit you are and how well equipped you are with clothing, survival kit, and tool kit.
4. Pocket-sized VHF transceivers, cell phones, personal locator beacons, satellite phones, hand-held GPS, and SPOT personal tracker offer some degree of safety, provided you know how and when to use them. A map and compass are still necessary tools for any wilderness traveller.
5. It is your responsibility to understand your machine to the extent that you can replace broken or worn parts in the field. Coincident with a basic knowledge of your engine is an understanding of your machine's behaviour in a wide range of snow and terrain conditions.
6. Thin ice and overflow pose a very serious threat to the safety of any overlander, especially if you have not taken a particular route before. Make sure to review the information on ice travel in Chapter 2.

Snowmobile Kit

- PSK
- spare drive belt
- spare spark plugs
- spare starter cord
- spare jets for carburetor
- spare bulb for headlight
- spare ignition key
- extra gasoline and two-cycle oil (750 millilitres, 267 fluid ounces)
- methyl hydrate
- compact snow shovel
- light tarpaulin
- axe
- snowshoes
- tool kit (appropriate for your machine)
- flashlight with alkaline or lithium batteries
- first-aid kit
- Thermos (with hot, sweet drink)
- magnetic screwdriver (to retrieve small parts dropped in snow)
- tow rope
- insulating pad
- sleeping bag

LIGHT FIXED-WING AIRCRAFT OR HELICOPTER GUIDE

Your safety in this instance is largely in the hands of the pilot, but that doesn't mean you should not be well equipped and informed of survival techniques.

In winter, even on a day flight, you should have a sleeping bag and a PSK with you.

The pilot should show you where the plane's Emergency Locator Transmitter (ELT) is located, as well as the company's survival kit.

Be aware of whether the pilot filed a flight note or a flight plan. The former is more open-ended.

Like in an automobile, the fuselage of an aircraft is a heat sink. If stranded, you should construct an emergency shelter if at all possible. If the aircraft is badly damaged, part of it can be used to make a shelter, especially if there is insufficient snow to construct a proper snow shelter. Cushions and fabric can be used as insulating pads or clothing.

If you are in a remote area, it is best to stay put. A downed or crashed aircraft is hard enough to find, but a person is much harder to spot.

Bush planes and helicopters should be equipped with a survival kit, an ELT, a snow shovel, an axe, and a first-aid kit.

Aircraft Passenger Kit

- PSK
- sleeping bag
- insulating pad
- light tarpaulin (pilot may have one)
- Thermos with hot, sweet drink
- snowshoes
- first-aid kit
- flashlight with alkaline or lithium batteries

Appendix B

SNOW TERMINOLOGY

PEOPLE INDIGENOUS TO THE polar regions, where snow plays such a significant part in their daily lives, have their own special vocabulary to describe the many different types of snow as well as the most common snow formations.

Inuktitut	English
anniu	snow
api	snow on the ground
qali	snow that collects on trees
upsik	wind-beaten snow
pukak	depth hoar
siqoq	drifting snow
saluma roaq	smooth snow surface or very fine particle
natatgonaq	rough snow surface of large particles
kimoaqruk	drift
siqoqtoaq	sun crust
anymanya	space formed between drift and obstruction causing it
kaioglaq (*sastrugi* or *skavler*)	sharply etched wind-eroded snow surface
tumarinyiq	irregular surface caused by differential erosion of hard and soft layers
qamaniq	bowl-shaped depression in snow around base of tree

ACKNOWLEDGEMENTS

TO MY PUBLISHER FOR recognizing that advances, predominantly in the field of electronics and the measurement of windchill, warranted a second edition.

To Jacqueline Carew and Gayle Alford for their computer assistance.

To Pat Mckenna for advice on the subject of food.

To my editor for her patience and probing queries.

SUGGESTED READING

Briggs, J.L. *Never in Anger.* Cambridge, MA: Harvard University Press, 1970.

Forgey, William W. *The Basic Essentials of Hypothermia.* Merryville, IN: ICS Books, Inc., 1991.

Forrester, Martyn. *Survival.* London: Sphere Books, 1987.

Halfpenny, James C., and Roy Douglas Ozanne. *Winter.* Boulder, CO: Johnson Books, 1989.

Perla, R.I., and M. Martinelli. *Avalanche Handbook.* (Agriculture Handbook 489.) Washington, DC: U.S. Department of Agriculture, Forest Service, 1975.

ABOUT THE AUTHOR

MONTY ALFORD IS A retired federal hydrographer who spent thirty-five years measuring and studying northern lakes and rivers. He is an experienced instructor of winter survival techniques and safe travel in snow and ice and a mountain guide who has made several ascents of northern peaks in Yukon, Alaska, and beyond. He is the author of five books and numerous articles in outdoor, northern, and geographical magazines. He lives in the Yukon.